Bible Wisdom to Improve Relationships

STAR Personality Styles

Volume II

The Best Things in Life
come from God
Do the Best you can with
the Talents that God has
given to You and
God will reward you with
The Best Things in Life.

With the Right Tools
and the Right Rules
it is possible to Achieve
Kingdom of Heaven on Earth

R. Luciani

Copyright © 2020

Publisher Disclaimer

The publisher of this book does not make any direct or indirect representation or warranties as to the claims made by the author nor endorse any of the products or services offered. The opinions and views expressed in this book belong to the author and may not be the opinions and views of the publishing company or affiliates.

Author Disclaimer

This book aims to share my opinions, experiences, and learning pertaining to personality styles with a focus on Holy Scripture from the Holy Bible and to improve relationships. This book is <u>not</u> intended to replace professional psychotherapy or counselling. This book is <u>not</u> intended to be used as instruction for parenting skills or caregiving. The thoughts that I share in this book are intended for normal adult relationship issues and are not intended to address the problems related to criminal activities.

Dedication

To my Lord God, who created me and gave me unconditional love.

To my Lord Holy Spirit, who guided and helped me through the tough times in life.

To my Lord Jesus Christ, who taught me how to become a Kingdom of Heaven STAR and gave his life so that I could be free of the original sin.

Most of the information that I share in this book comes from the Holy Bible, my observations and conversations that I have had with others. I believe that the Holy Spirit has guided me to fine-tune my teachings to be better organized and more complete than I have shared in past conversations. Glory be to my Lord God, my Lord Holy Spirit, and my Lord Jesus Christ, who have guided the words that I share.

To my Four-Dimension STAR wife, Roxana, without whom this book could not have been completed.

To my first-born miracle: Kristofor.

To my second-born miracle: Angela.

To my third-born miracle: Nikolas.

To you, the reader, thank you for joining me on this journey and welcome. I pray that the information that I share with you in this book will have a godly benefit to you.

INTROVERTED
PEOPLE
TASK
EXTROVERTED

Contents

Volume II xiii

    Tools and Rules xiii

Praise for Bible Wisdom to Improve Relationships.... xv

    Reverend Ron Mainse of A Better Us xv

        STAR - Personality-Styles (Complete) xv

    Sam Ibeh of the Online Book Club...................... xvii

        STAR - Personality-Styles (Complete) xvii

    Heena R. Pardeshi of The Reading Bud xix

        STAR Personality Styles (Complete)................ xix

        STAR Personality Styles (Volume 1)................ xix

        STAR Personality Styles (Volume 2)................ xx

Acknowledgements xxiii

Preface to Volume II xxvii

    My Writing Style xxix

        The Message Versus Grammar xxx

        Capitalization.................................... xxx

        Inefficiency of Expression........................ xxxii

        Minor Word Usage xxxiv

        Humour can Cause Confusion.....................xxxv

        I like Precision of Language......................xxxv

        My Many Years of Programming.................. xxxvi

        New Term Abbreviations xxxviii

Introduction 1

STAR Personality Styles is For Everyone 3

Section 4 – Dealing with RATS 5

16. Dealing with RATSs and Crazy-Makers 7

17. Quality Communication 19

Albert Mehrabian's 7-38-55 Rule 19

Active Listening 19

Flattery Versus Edification 21

The Four Horsemen 25

Personality Styles' and Messages 34

18. Conflict 37

Five Stages of Grief 48

Fight, Flight, Freeze, Or Fix 52

Two Ears, Two Eyes, and One Mouth 52

19. Resolving Conflicts 61

Add God and Stir 64

20. How to Fight Fair 79

DESK - Setting the Foundation 82

DESK Goal, Preparation and Execution 83

D.E.S.K. 85

DESK from the Holy Bible 88

DESK Scenarios 90

DESK and the Sufferer 91

DESK and the Trespasser 96

DESK Brainstorming 99

21. RATS, Grow Up Or Be Left Behind 101

22. Overcoming RATS Syndrome 119

Introduction to Biblical Duties 123

One Life and Then Judgment 125

Section 5 – From the Bible............................. 129

23. Power of Prayer 131

First Prayer Miracle.................................. 135

Second Prayer Miracle 136

Third Prayer Miracle 136

Fourth Prayer Miracle............................... 138

Fifth Prayer Miracle 139

Sixth Prayer Miracle................................ 142

Seventh Prayer Miracle 143

A Bonus Miracle Story.............................. 144

Another Bonus Miracle Story...................... 144

24. Message to Husbands and Wives.................... 145

Equally Yoked Husband and Wife 145

Unequally Yoked Husband and Wife............... 156

Husband and Wife and Submission................. 163

25. Relationship Laws from the Bible 165

What is Love?....................................... 166

What Love is Not.................................... 168

Jesus Teaches Us How to Love 169

The Lord's Prayer:................................... 170

Relationships in General............................. 171

Relationships With God and Others 180

Duty to God Overrides Everything Else........... 184

The Golden Rule..................................... 186

Always Do the Right Thing For Strangers 187

Our Duty as Christians 189

Let Not Your Good Be Evil Spoken of 190

Judge Not, Lest Ye Be Judged........................ 190

Loving Strange Women (Or Men)..................... 192

Marriage is... 195

Wife's Duty to Her Husband 197

Husband's Duty to His Wife 208

Sexual Duties.. 218

Grounds For Divorce 218

Divorce 222

Father's and Mother's Duties 223

Children's Duty to Parents 228

Neighbour's Duties to Neighbours 231

Sex Laws 232

Creditor / Government Duties 235

Master's Duty to Servant................................ 242

Servant's Duty to Master:............................... 245

Our Duty to Our Enemies............................... 246

Speak Only Words of Edification...................... 249

When Someone Sins Against You...................... 250

Forgiveness.. 250

Grace and Pardon Must Be Earned................... 255

Appendix xxxvii

The Art of the STAR Apology........................ xxxix

Releasing and Expressing Anger – Safely xli

No More Faking-fine xlvii

Prayer: Love, Joy, Peace, and Harmony xlix

STAR Personality Styles Are Fluid......................liii

The Impact of Free Will On Personality Styles.. liii

Summary of My Personality Style Changes:....... liv

Impact of Word Alive Press lviii

Warning to New Christian Authors xciv

Index xcvii

Disclaimer xcix

About the Author ci

My Four Hundred Pound Stone ciii

Final messages cvii

Share your Stories cviii

Identify your Kingdom Assignment cviii

Make Life Easier for You cviii

Thank you for reading my book cix

Consider Leaving a Book Review cx

I Promise to Read your Review cxi

Volume II

Tools and Rules

With the Right Tools
and the Right Rules
it is possible to Achieve
Kingdom of Heaven on Earth
R. Luciani

Praise for Bible Wisdom to Improve Relationships

Originally printed under title STAR Personality Styles

Reverend Ron Mainse of A Better Us

https://www.abetterus.tv/

STAR - Personality-Styles (Complete)

STAR Personality Styles, is a great resource, especially for married couples who must learn to understand and appreciate each other's personality differences in order to enjoy a happy marriage. Using powerful principles from the Bible, the author explains both positive and negative personality styles and offers practical advice for effectively resolving conflicts. The book also encourages readers to overcome negative personality traits within themselves, thus promoting personal growth and self-awareness.

STAR Personality Styles is written in an easy-to-understand language that is accessible to all readers, and the book's principles are applicable in all interpersonal relationships, including marriage, family, friends, and colleagues.

I would recommend STAR Personality Styles as a valuable resource for anyone looking to dive deeper into understanding their own personality style and effectively using that knowledge toward building a better relationship with those closest to them.

Rev. Ron Mainse
President of Heart to Heart Marriage & Family Ministries
Host of "A Better Us" Television

Sam Ibeh of the Online Book Club

https://forums.onlinebookclub.org/

STAR - Personality-Styles (Complete)

https://forums.onlinebookclub.org/viewtopic.php?f=24&t=234796

4 out of 4 stars

STAR – Personality Styles is a self-help and spiritual book. It's a two-volume book and a summation of R. Luciani's past experiences with people and how they correlate with godly living.

R. Luciani explained the need for God in our personal lives to make us better humans, spiritually and emotionally.

Humans have always been curious about understanding their psyche. There have also been different personality classifications, like the popularly known Myers & Briggs' "16-Personality Test." R. Luciani advocated the STAR personality because of its simplification.

A backbone of this book was the continuous linkage of his teachings to Jesus Christ. The scriptural verses were written in Old English, reminiscent of Shakespearean plays. This might break comprehension for those unfamiliar with such words because the verses were a significant part of the book. The author's writing style might be a bit novel because of his capitalization and emphasis on maintaining his unique sentence delivery. He clarified that, though.

During my reading, I had to do a lot of self-reflection. The book would make you go on a slow pace for better digestion of messages, or else you might get information overload. Accentuating that personality style is never rigid and is adjusted based on one's current situation and desires is my best lesson learned in the book. The author also highlighted the positive and negative attributes of each.

R. Luciani

The reverse of STAR, RATS, and CM (Crazy Makers) were humorous. Concrete examples could be seen in the stories of his life and the biblical examples of Jesus' escapades. The author asserted that Jesus was the perfect example of the four personality types, and he urged us to emulate him to the best of our abilities.

The second volume's central theme was conflict resolution and human relationships. There, the author provided a lot of enlightening lessons. I was reminded that conflicts were bound to arise in every human interaction, and how they would be dealt with would determine their longevity. The author's life wasn't easy, as could be seen from his childhood, divorce fiasco, and various life trials and tribulations.

STAR – Personality Styles is a wonderful book. I'm not overly religious, but I can appreciate the author's zeal to spread the word of God. He says it is his kingdom's assignment, and his belief in God is reinforced daily by this tradition. He urges us to enjoy the process of our natural life. He provides links for the reader to share their stories, which can also help others in their life journey.

Considering the thorough editing process (without errors) and content-filled information, I'd rate STAR Personality Styles 4 out of 4 stars. I had nothing significant to dislike, and I would recommend it primarily to Christians. Also, readers of self-help and psychology books would find it interesting.

Heena R. Pardeshi of The Reading Bud

https://thereadingbud.com/

STAR Personality Styles (Complete)

https://thereadingbud.com/2022/06/10/book-review-star-personality-styles-volume-1-star-and-rats-rats-grow-up-or-be-left-behind-by-r-luciani/

5 out of 5 stars

This book is a complete package with the first volume providing insights to the readers about the relationship mechanisms and context into how exactly people's minds work while being in relationships and dealing with them and the second book giving a detailed look into conflict resolution and various solutions related to relationship problems. The author uses examples, anecdotes and teachings from the Bible in order to present his ideas but he has done so in such a way that even if you are not a Christian and have not read the Bible it'll all make perfect sense to you.

The author's writing has a beautiful flow and the style of writing resonated with me. I was able to read this book very easily and without any difficulty related to the pacing of the prose.

This combined book is great for anyone looking to understand the "why" behind human psychology of relationships and also the "what to do" in case they find themselves facing a related problem.

STAR Personality Styles (Volume 1)

https://thereadingbud.com/2022/06/10/book-review-star-personality-styles-volume-1-star-and-rats-rats-grow-up-or-be-left-behind-by-r-luciani/

5 out of 5 stars

STAR Personality Styles (Vol.1: STARS And RATS) RATS: Grow Up Or Be Left Behind by R. Luciani is a brilliant and insightful book about the workings of people's personalities and their relationships. R. Luciani has highlighted the types of personalities and the ways to deal with such personalities in his latest 2-volume book series, STAR Personality Styles using his knowledge of the Bible to draw parallels and to define personalities and the ways to handle the negative ones.

I am a firm believer that religious texts are mostly written keeping in mind a common man and how this common man can overcome obstacles in their daily life and live happily. Cementing on this belief, I had the privilege to get the opportunity to read and review books by author R. Luciani who draws heavily from the Holy Bible to explain and describe different kinds of people around us and how their personalities bare an influence on their relationships, especially marriage – the most sacred of all relationships.

STAR Personality Styles (Volume 2)

https://thereadingbud.com/2022/07/07/book-review-star-personality-styles-volume-2-tools-rules-rats-grow-up-or-be-left-behind-by-r-luciani/

5 out of 5 stars

STAR Personality Styles (Vol.2: TOOLS & RULES) RATS: Grow Up Or Be Left Behind by R. Luciani is the second volume to STAR Personality Styles (Vol.1: STARS & RATS) RATS: Grow Up Or Be Left Behind. This book goes further in exploring the relationship dynamics between two people and explains ways to effectively resolve conflicts.

Author R. Luciani again draws largely from the Holy Bible to explain and describe ways in which relationship conflicts can be easily resolved with a little patience and understanding. I found the concepts explained in his book very helpful and feel positive that they would help others greatly too.

I would definitely recommend this book to anyone who is going through a difficult time in their relationship and needs help, advice or is seeking direction in general.

INTROVERTED
PEOPLE
TASK
EXTROVERTED

Acknowledgements

The Holy Bible, of course, stands apart as the greatest of all sources of knowledge. However, I am an avid reader and I have studied under many good teachers. A few teachers stand out as excellent and deserving of mention. My teachings are different from others, though, because my experiences and perceptions colour my teachings. The following are some books and teachers who have had a significant impact on my knowledge about personality styles and relationships:

- The Holy Bible (King James Version)
- Sword Searcher software (https://www.swordsearcher.com/)
  - All KJV and WEB verses in this book are sourced from the SwordSearcher program.
  - All Webster's 1828 Dictionary definitions in this book are sourced from the SwordSearcher program.
  - All Webster's Revised Unabridged Dictionary 1913 definitions in this book are sourced from the SwordSearcher program.
- Webster's 1828 Dictionary
  - is the best source for comprehending the old English used in the Holy Bible (KJV)
- Dr. Charles Stanley
  Television Broadcast
  - Dr. Charles Stanley explains how to establish the best relationship possible with God.
- Pastor Andy Stanley
  Television Broadcast
  - Pastor Andy Stanley is excellent at explaining how some of the best conventional wisdom is rooted in wisdom from the Holy Bible.
- Dr. David Jeremiah

> Television Broadcast
>   - o Dr. David Jeremiah is great at unpacking principles of truth in the Holy Bible and explaining how the Old and New Testaments are closely linked.

- A Better Us
  > Television Broadcast
  >   - o Ron & Ann Mainse lead 'Kitchen couples' in discussions to share information that will lead to better marriages.
- Dr. Rob Reimer (author of Soul Care)
  > Published by Carpenter's Son Publishing, Franklin, Tennessee
  > Published in association with Larry Carpenter of Christian Book Services, LLC
  >   - o Dr. Rob Reimer does a great job explaining the steps to protect and care for your soul.
- Robert A. Rohm, Ph.D. (author of Positive Personality Profiles)
  > Published by Personality Insights, Inc.
  > Post Office Box 28592
  > Atlanta, Georgia 30358-0592
  >   - o This book has an excellent section on how to motivate individuals based on their individual personality style
- Pastor Gary Thomas (author of When to Walk Away)
  > Published in association with Yates & Yates
  > 1551 N. Tustin Ave., Suite 710
  > Santa Ana, California 92705
  >   - o I dog-ear important pages when I read, and there are many dog-eared pages after reading Gary Thomas' book "When to Walk Away."
- Brian D. McLaren (author of The Secret Message of Jesus)
  > Published by W Publishing Group,

A division of Thomas Nelson, Inc.,
P.O. Box 141000,
Nashville, Tennessee 37214

- o The message of Jesus is far broader than most people comprehend when reading the four New Testament Gospels.

- John Gottman (the Four Horsemen: Criticism, Defensiveness, Contempt, Stonewalling)
  - o I have not yet read any of John Gottman's books, but I like the simplicity of his list of the four horsemen.

Preface to Volume II

STAR Personality Styles was written as one single book; however, because of the amount of information included, the book became too large for the standard paperback format, so I split the book into two volumes. Several books in the Holy Bible contain a large volume of information that was too large for the Greek Scroll Format and were consequently split into Two Books. Likewise, the information contained in the STAR Personality Styles is too large for the Paperback Format and is consequently divided into two volumes. I recommend that both volumes be read as one book to get the full benefit.

To ensure the best comprehension and value to you, the reader, I highly recommend reading Volume I before reading Volume II.

All beneficial, effective and righteous wisdom, understanding, and knowledge, originally comes from God through prophets and godly people. Somewhere along the way, scientists decided to reject God, however, many of the scientists of the past were Godly people. When I was a child, I enjoyed reading fiction; when I became a young adult, I rarely read fiction, and I developed a strong desire for non-fiction in my attempt to comprehend the world around me. The information that I gained was useless until I incorporated the information into my knowledge to expand my wisdom. As I travelled through my life journey, in a world where people use words to tear down rather than to build up, the path did not change, but the scenery did. Often the scenery became more vibrant as I discovered books and knowledge that supported and enhanced my established beliefs and comprehension of my world.

The books that I enjoy most are the books that tell me that the information that I had already learned (from the Holy Bible) is true and correct. The experience of having books corroborate my knowledge is not surprising since my favourite book is the Holy Bible and the source of so many of the books that I read. I validate all information presented to me by comparing the new information to God's Holy Word as found in the Holy Bible. I consider the King James Version of the Holy Bible to be the ultimate authority of truth and wisdom, and scientific discoveries do not invalidate the Holy Bible. I have found that different authors read the Holy Bible from different perspectives and, by reading their books about wisdom from the Holy Bible, I have learned new and different Godly wisdom. I might not always agree with their perspectives; however, since disagreements in interpretation require investigation, I have increased my wisdom, understanding, and knowledge of the teachings of the Holy Bible.

I started writing this book, and other books not yet published, more than thirty years ago. In my mid-thirties, I started collecting verses from the Holy Bible into Wisdom Topics. I only shared my collection with family and friends. In this book, I share the wisdom that I have gained, focusing on relationships. Since my early twenties, I have been an avid reader of non-fiction, close to forty years now. The 'source' of much of my knowledge is now forgotten, and the information itself has become part of my knowledge base. As with everyone, I was born without any knowledge worthy of writing a book; however, I have collected knowledge over the years through experience, reading, and education.

My Writing Style

After receiving several comments about my writing style in this book and my previous experiences with many participants in my teachings on this subject, I felt it might be helpful to include an explanation of my writing style.

Though it might not be of much comfort to my readers, it is comforting to me to know that I share a similar challenging vocabulary and writing style as found in the King James Version of the Holy Bible. My unusual style most likely resulted from reading the King James Version of the Holy Bible for most of my life.

Many modern-English versions of the Holy Bible hide Paul's challenging writing style with liberal interpretations; however, if you read the King James Version of the Holy Bible, the challenges of his writing style are more evident. Like Paul, I also have a quirky and challenging writing style.

One of the challenges of reading the Epistles of Paul is that not only was the King James Version written in Old English, but Paul was also trained to be an expert Pharisee (an expert in law, a lawyer). He was taught to speak and write using Term of Art or what modern English might call legalese.

Studying the King James Version of the Epistles of Paul gives the student an advantage in reading legal documents today. They both require slow, careful reading with special dictionaries and meticulous study to comprehend the intended messages.

I often describe my writing style as being similar to the Pharisee-Apostle Paul in the Holy Bible. Paul did not have a copy editor. Before my writings were copyedited, many people told me that my writings were as challenging to comprehend as the Apostle Paul's.

Though unrelated to writing style, another similarity to Paul is that Paul wrote many letters while in prison when there was nothing else he could do. I started writing my books during

COVID and the Economic Aftermath of COVID when there was nothing else that I could do.

The Message Versus Grammar

The following verse from the Holy Bible is one sentence. From the beginning of this sentence to the end of this sentence, there is only one period. Using today's copyediting standards, a copyeditor would rewrite this single sentence into many sentences and probably several paragraphs.

> *Colossians 1:21-29 (KJV) And you, that were sometime alienated and enemies in your mind by wicked works, yet now hath he reconciled In the body of his flesh through death, to present you holy and unblameable and unreproveable in his sight: If ye continue in the faith grounded and settled, and be not moved away from the hope of the gospel, which ye have heard, and which was preached to every creature which is under heaven; whereof I Paul am made a minister; Who now rejoice in my sufferings for you, and fill up that which is behind of the afflictions of Christ in my flesh for his body's sake, which is the church: Whereof I am made a minister, according to the dispensation of God which is given to me for you, to fulfil the word of God; Even the mystery which hath been hid from ages and from generations, but now is made manifest to his saints: To whom God would make known what is the riches of the glory of this mystery among the Gentiles; which is Christ in you, the hope of glory: Whom we preach, warning every man, and teaching every man in all wisdom; that we may present every man perfect in Christ Jesus: Whereunto I also labour, striving according to his working, which worketh in me mightily.*

Like many of the authors of the King James Version of the Holy Bible, I tend to focus more on the message than on technical writing style.

Capitalization

It is uncommon or unusual to use Capitalization in the middle of the sentence (as opposed to the beginning of the sentence); however, it is considered acceptable to use Capitalization within the sentence when Capitalization is used to denote a "Title of Respect" such as "Your Honour" or "His Honour" when you are speaking to, or referring to, a judge. Rather than demote everyone down to the level of a commoner, I will often raise the "Title of Respect" of a commoner to a level equal to nobility, so I use "Line-Labourer" as a Title of Respect equivalent to "Her Majesty." I believe that it is more important to see people as who they are on God's Earth than in Man's World.

A "Title of Respect" is similar to the "personification of an abstract" in law. When a lawyer "addresses the Court," he actually addresses the judge. The lawyer might also use the Title of Respect of "Your Honour" when speaking to the judge.

I sometimes use Capitalization in the middle of a sentence to emphasize an abstract concept, character or idea in an ideal sense as if it existed as a material object.

Using Capitalization in the middle of a sentence is uncommon, or unusual, but it is considered acceptable when personifying a metonymic. When referring to Jesus as a Role Model, I am using Jesus' characteristic of role model as a personified metonymic, in a manner similar to using the word "ride" as a metonymic for "car." Because Jesus is a proper noun, the metonymic Role Model is also capitalized. Because the term car is not a proper noun and is written in lowercase, the metonymic ride is lowercase.

I must admit that my Technical STAR Personality Style found a rule to explain and justify what I do subconsciously and automatically without thinking. If I were to consciously and purposely use Capitalization as a Metonymic, I would capitalize He and Him every time I referred to God, Holy Spirit, and Jesus. The King James Version of the Holy Bible does not capitalize He or Him. The Holy Bible describes both Holy Spirit and Jesus as ministers, helpers, and servants to the Righteous; Christians elevate Jesus to a superior position, but Jesus did not expressly elevate himself.

You are correct if you thought to yourself that my Technical STAR Personality Style found another rule to explain and justify what I do subconsciously and automatically, without

R. Luciani

thinking. My Relationship STAR Personality Style admits the truth to you, the Reader, in a humorous manner. Be thankful that I do not use CamelCase, which is very common in Java programming. ☺.

Inefficiency of Expression

I developed a style of *inefficiency of expression* because of the many examples in the Holy Bible of verses like "He said … and he said …, and he said …" where it can sometimes become challenging to know who is saying what to whom. For example, verses Psalm 55:17-22:

Psalm 55:9-23 (KJV) **Destroy, O Lord, and divide their tongues**: for I have seen violence and strife in the city. **Day and night they go about it upon the walls thereof**: mischief also and sorrow are in the midst of it. **Wickedness is in the midst thereof: deceit and guile depart not from her streets.** For **it was not an enemy that reproached me; then I could have borne it: neither was it he that hated me that did magnify himself against me; then I would have hid myself from him**: But it was **thou, a man mine equal, my guide, and mine acquaintance. We took sweet counsel together, and walked unto the house of God in company**. Let death seize upon them, and let them go down quick into hell: for wickedness is in their dwellings, and among them. **As for me, I will call upon God; and the LORD shall save me**. Evening, and morning, and at noon, will I pray, and cry aloud: and **he** shall hear my voice. **He** hath delivered my soul in peace from the battle that was against me: for there were many with me. God shall hear, and afflict them, even **he** that abideth of old. Selah. Because they have no changes, therefore they fear not God. **He** hath put forth **his** hands **against such as be at peace with him**: **he** hath broken **his** covenant. The words of **his** mouth were smoother than butter, but war was in **his** heart: **his** words were softer than oil, yet were they drawn swords. Cast thy burden upon the LORD, and **he** shall sustain thee: **he** shall never suffer the righteous to be moved. **But thou, O God, shalt bring them down into the pit of destruction: bloody and deceitful men shall not live out half their days; but I will trust in thee**. [Emphasis added]

In Psalm 55, David is experiencing the tribulation of rejection from someone that he trusted. David calls on God for help and then describes the tribulation that he is experiencing. Sometimes "he" and "his" refer to God, and sometimes "he" and "his" refer to David's betrayer friend. David ends the Psalm with "But thou, oh God … but I will trust in thee," so we can determine that the "evil he" refers to the betrayer friend and the "good he" refers to God. I prefer to use some inefficient redundancy to ensure better comprehension by replacing he, him, she, her, they, and them with the name(s) of the individual(s).

Psalm 89:1-7 (KJV) Maschil of Ethan the Ezrahite. I will sing of the mercies of the LORD for ever: with my mouth will I make known thy faithfulness to all generations. For I have said, Mercy shall be built up for ever: thy faithfulness shalt thou establish in the very heavens. I have made a covenant with my chosen, I have sworn unto David my servant, Thy seed will I establish for ever, and build up thy throne to all generations. Selah. And the heavens shall praise thy wonders, O LORD: thy faithfulness also in the congregation of the saints. For who in the heaven can be compared unto the LORD? who among the sons of the mighty can be likened unto the LORD? God is greatly to be feared in the assembly of the saints, and to be had in reverence of all them that are about him.

Another example of the Confusion caused by using simple pronouns can be found in Psalm 89:1-7 (KJV), in which sometimes "I" refers to Maschil of Ethan the Ezrahite speaking, and sometimes "I" refers to God speaking. You can only determine who is speaking by examining the surrounding context of spoken words.

*1 Samuel 15:35 (KJV) And **Samuel came no more to see Saul until the day of his death**: nevertheless Samuel mourned for Saul: and the LORD repented that he had made Saul king over Israel.*

Every time I read 1 Samuel 15:35, I *initially* comprehend that Samuel no longer came to see Saul until Saul's death. Each time, I need to remind myself that Samuel died <u>before</u> Saul

R. Luciani

(refer to 1 Samuel 28); therefore, the death refers to Samuel's death and not Saul's death. I would have written the verse as "And Samuel came no more to see Saul until the day of Samuel's death:" so that the sentence would have been more straight-forward.

Here is one for those of you with an interesting sense of humour. Please believe me when I explain that I mean no disrespect to the Holy Bible. I share this only to explain my unusual writing style.

> *2 Kings 19:35 (KJV) And it came to pass that night, that the angel of the LORD went out, and smote in the camp of the Assyrians an hundred fourscore and five thousand: and **when they arose early in the morning**, behold, **they were all dead corpses**.*

When *they* arose in the morning, *they* were dead. Is this where Hollywood came up with the Zombie Apocalypse Genre? ☺.

Minor Word Usage

Webster's Revised Unabridged Dictionary 1913 defines Understand with several nuances; one definition component is "To stand under; to support."

The term "understanding" has an additional meaning of taking a position or standing under the position or standing of another; therefore, I prefer to use the term comprehend or comprehension in most cases. Though there is no difference between the terms in common usage, there is a slight difference in definitions. I like *precision of language*, so I will use the terms comprehend or comprehension, whereas most authors would use the terms "understand" or "understanding."

The term "want" is another term with an uncommon meaning. The term "want," as used in the Holy Bible, usually means "a lack of," so there is essentially no difference between the phrases "I want a million dollars" and "I lack a million dollars." Since the term "want," when used in the Holy Bible KJV, means "lack," I choose to use the term desire instead of the term want in most cases or modern comprehension.

Humour can Cause Confusion

My friends, who are used to my sense of humour, know that I will often say things that seem to be unreligious. I sat with one friend for several hours, discussing the Holy Bible. When we discussed my Wisdom Topics collection, I announced, "I am writing the Third Testament of the Holy Bible." My friend said, "I know you, so I know you do not disrespect the Bible, so what is the Third Testament?". I told him about my project to collect every verse of the Holy Bible into Wisdom Topics.

While sitting with another friend, talking about the Holy Bible, I commented, "I am always lucky." My friend has heard this un-biblical statement often and knew that I meant that God continually protects and blesses me.

I like Precision of Language

All communication between any two people will be somewhat challenging. This challenge has been true throughout the Holy Bible. There are always many obstacles to full comprehension when any two people communicate with each other. The efforts of any author to write in a manner that the Reader will comprehend is always challenging. Many people involved in conversations with me have heard me apologize for miscommunicating and causing Confusion.

I have heard several stereotypes about the correlation between intelligence and clarity of message; the clarity of the message increases with the speaker's intelligence. Personally, I have found that intelligent people can be as incoherent as unintelligent people. I no longer believe that a lack of intelligence is an accurate label to describe the cause of Confusion in communication.

The brain can think of many thoughts/messages in the time that it takes to speak a single message. Some people are better (or more patient) at organizing their thoughts into words than others. It is easier for me to write my thoughts than to speak my thoughts. In the written medium, my thoughts are forced to slow down to accommodate my slow fingers, and I can edit and rewrite my thoughts until my written thoughts are at least easier to comprehend.

I like *precision of language*; however, most people do not usually speak or comprehend communication in my *precision of language*. I have noticed three common failures on my part when I speak to people that I know:

1. I will speak in their Commonly used language and be misunderstood and
2. I will speak in my Precision of Language and be misunderstood, and
3. I will speak part of a message, abandon the message mid-thought because my mind has changed to another thought, continue speaking part of another message, and be misunderstood.

I have learned to over-explain in an effort to have my message be comprehended more clearly. Please be patient with my Precision of Language while reading my book's messages. If you can easily comprehend my message, the Holy Spirit has helped you comprehend <u>my</u> gobbledygook. I wish the Holy Spirit would explain to the birds that they can eat the cherries at the top of my cherry tree, that they should leave the lower hanging fruit for me to collect, and that the birds should stop pecking at the cherries before they are ripe. I tried to tell the birds, but they ignored my words. ☺.

My Many Years of Programming

I choose to blame my writing style's challenges on my intellect and my many years of programming. Programming is like speaking a foreign language with a computer.

In my mid-twenties, I applied for an Information Technology Manager position in a company where I had already proven my ability to take on and achieve new challenges. While in university, I achieved excellent grades in some obscure programming classes, but I had no relevant training or programming experience pertinent to the company's requirements; they were concerned about the need to train me. Therefore, the company executives insisted that I undergo Intellectual and Emotional Intelligence tests. I scored at the '92 Percentile' on the Intellectual Intelligence Test and 'Very High' on the Emotional Intelligence Test.

For those of you who prefer using the standard IQ Score, I scored 122, but this number does not make sense to my Technical Personality Style. Someone told me that an IQ Score of 140 is a "genius" level, and I have heard that an IQ score of 222 is the highest recorded IQ Score. If we look at 122 in ratio to 140, then we have a value of about 87%. If we look at 122 in ratio to 222, then we have a value of about 50%. It is much easier to measure based on a scale of 100, so I know that when I scored at the 92 percentile, I was in the top 8%.

The psychiatrist who conducted the test advised me that, because of my intelligence, I would need to make extra effort to clarify my message to listeners and not assume that everyone understands my message without clarification.

Though I later learned that the psychiatrist was correct, I have also found that the opposite is true – I sometimes have difficulty comprehending simple things because I often overthink things.

I believe that my high score of 92 percentile in the intellectual intelligence test is simply due to my thinking patterns being changed by the Holy Spirit.

*Isaiah 11:2-3 And the **spirit of the LORD** shall rest upon him, the spirit of **wisdom** and **understanding**, the spirit of **counsel** and **might**, the spirit of **knowledge** and of the **fear** of the LORD; And **shall make him of quick understanding** in the fear of the LORD: and **he shall not judge after the sight of his eyes, neither reprove after the hearing of his ears**:*

I don't believe that my intellect results from my physical brain. The Holy Spirit is quicker and more intelligent than the human brain.

I did not get the position of I.T. Manager that I had applied for. Instead, I was offered a position as a Computer Analyst – working with Computer Users to define Program Requirements in order to design Program Logic for programmers to code. The company executives found that I could see the small details of a plan and how the details fit into the overall goal or purpose of the plan; combining this ability with my high level of empathy made me very effective as a Computer Analyst.

New Term Abbreviations

Usually, I dislike using abbreviations because they require the Reader to learn a new language. However, abbreviations are quicker and more efficient to type; therefore, some new abbreviation terms might be introduced later in this book.

Introduction

STAR Personality Styles is For Everyone

STAR Personality Styles was written as one single book; however, because of the amount of information included, the book became too large for the standard paperback format, so I split the book into two volumes. Several books in the Holy Bible contain a large volume of information that was too large for the Greek Scroll Format and were consequently split into Two Books. Likewise, the information contained in the STAR Personality Styles is too large for the Paperback Format and is consequently divided into two volumes. I recommend that both volumes be read as one book to get the full benefit.

I am close to sixty years old, so I have decided to complete two of my long-time goals: writing books and growing my beard to chest length☺. In my younger years, I served the needs of many companies on a Contract-for-hire basis. I worked with Large Companies and Small Companies. I worked with CEOs and Line-Labourers. I worked with Muslims, Jews, Christians, Buddhists, Agnostics, and Atheists. I worked with men and women (both heterosexual and homosexual). I worked with Africans, Americans, Brazilians, Britons, Canadians, Chinese, Indians, Italians, Japanese, Mexicans, Romanians, and people from several other countries. I worked with Pessimists and Optimists. I have had long conversations with Pastors, Ministers, Priests, Deacons, Rabbis, Shamans, Monks, and Yogis. The information within "STAR Personality Styles" works in each of these relationships. The information within this STAR Personality Style is intended for improving comprehension of relationships between mentally competent adults and is not intended to be used as Parenting or Caregiving Advice.

Section 4 – Dealing with RATS

INTROVERTED
PEOPLE
TASK
EXTROVERTED
R

16. Dealing with RATSs and Crazy-Makers

When you argue, do you argue about details or feelings? When your opponent argues, do they argue about details or feelings? The answer to these two questions will help you determine whether you or your opponent have a task-oriented personality style or a people-oriented personality style.

When you argue, do you yell loudly with a lot of passion or yell quietly with an insulting tone of voice? When your opponent argues, do they yell loudly with a lot of passion or yell quietly with an insulting tone of voice? The answer to these two questions will help you determine whether you or your opponent are extroverted or introverted.

When you argue, do you threaten any violence? When your opponent argues, do they threaten any violence? An Action RATS is the most likely to initiate a threat of violence, so answering these two questions will determine whether you or your opponent is an Action RATS.

When dealing with RATSs or Crazy-Makers, don't put your confidence in your ability to resolve the conflict. Instead, put your confidence in God's Ability to guide the RATSs or Crazy-Makers to become STARs. In the appendix, I have included a prayer that I often use.

Proverbs 29:9 (KJV) If a wise man [or woman] contendeth with a foolish man [or woman], whether he [or she] rage or laugh, there is no rest. [Clarification terms added]

Proverbs 15:18 (KJV) A wrathful man [or woman] stirreth up strife: but he [or she] that is slow to anger appeaseth strife. [Clarification terms added]

The Holy Bible has wise instructions for every situation. Proverbs teaches how to deal with others who are not our spiritual equals.

16. Dealing with RATSs and Crazy-Makers

Like a magician using smoke and mirrors, all RATSs and Crazy-Makers use gaslighting to cause deception. The style of the deception changes with the different negative personality styles. However, your response to the RATSs and Crazy-Makers should always remain the same:

1. Recognize the pattern of distortion (blend of truth and lie) or deception (total lie).
2. Recognize the weakness that is being used against you.
3. Use Holy Scripture (such as God loves me as I am) as a protective barrier to keep yourself focused on a godly emotions-based response instead of a natural feelings-based reaction. Do not engage in blame or defence.
4. *If* you cannot calmly deal with the conflict, *then* walk away from the temptation. Walk away to another room, outside the house, or go for a drive, etc.

Remember that <u>all</u> STARs will sometimes have a bad day and behave like RATSs. Don't apply the label of RATS for a rare, out-of-character unpleasant behaviour.

Galatians 6:1 (KJV) Brethren, if a man be overtaken in a fault, ye which are spiritual, restore such an one in the spirit of meekness; considering thyself, lest thou also be tempted.

2 Corinthians 10:5 (KJV) Casting down imaginations, and every high thing that exalteth itself against the knowledge of God, and bringing into captivity every thought to the obedience of Christ;

Proverbs 4:23-24 (KJV) Keep [Guard] thy heart with all diligence; for out of it are the issues of life. Put away from thee a froward [stubborn, unyielding] mouth, and perverse lips put far from thee. [Clarifying terms added]

The Holy Bible cautions that if we apply the label of RATS or Crazy-Maker to someone's trespass, we might be tempted to react with typical RATS or Crazy-Maker behaviour. This common feelings-based reaction will escalate the conflict. To de-escalate the conflict, the participants must calmly contemplate the situation with a godly mind, heart, and will.

As a programmer, I found that computer users typically jumped to conclusions, which led me down the wrong path of investigating a wrong section of code. I learned to do my due diligence to determine the true facts before I started my investigation so that I could recommend a good and correct solution.

When dealing with RATS or Crazy-Maker, do not accept their statements as truth; do your due diligence and determine the true facts so that you can respond righteously to their trespass.

1 Corinthians 8:1-13 (KJV) Now as touching things offered unto idols, we know that we all have knowledge. Knowledge puffeth up, but charity edifieth. And if any man think that he knoweth any thing, he knoweth nothing yet as he ought to know. But if any man love God, the same is known of him. As concerning therefore the eating of those things that are offered in sacrifice unto idols, we know that an idol is nothing in the world, and that there is none other God but one. For though there be that are called gods, whether in heaven or in earth, (as there be gods many, and lords many,) But to us there is but one God, the Father, of whom are all things, and we in him; and one Lord Jesus Christ, by whom are all things, and we by him. Howbeit there is not in every man that knowledge: for some with conscience of the idol unto this hour eat it as a thing offered unto an idol; and their conscience being weak is defiled. But meat commendeth us not to God: for neither, if we eat, are we the better; neither, if we eat not, are we the worse. But take heed lest by any means this liberty of yours become a stumblingblock to them that are weak. For if any man see thee which hast knowledge sit at meat in the idol's temple, shall not the conscience of him which is weak be emboldened to eat those things which are offered to idols; And through thy knowledge shall the weak brother perish, for whom Christ died? But when ye sin so against the brethren, and wound their weak conscience, ye sin against Christ. Wherefore, if meat make my brother to offend, I will eat no flesh while the world standeth, lest I make my brother to offend.

1 Timothy 2:1-6 (KJV) I exhort therefore, that, first of all, supplications, prayers, intercessions, and giving of thanks, be made for all men; For kings, and for all that are in authority; that we may lead a quiet and peaceable life in all godliness and honesty. For this is good and acceptable in the sight of God our Saviour; Who will have all men to be saved, and to come unto the knowledge of the truth. For there is one God, and one mediator between God and men, the man Christ Jesus; Who gave himself a ransom for all, to be testified in due time.

1 Corinthians 7:33-34 (KJV) But he that is married careth for the things that are of the world, how he may please his wife. There is difference also between a wife and a virgin. The unmarried woman careth for the things of the Lord, that she may be holy both in body and in spirit: but she that is married careth for the things of the world, how she may please her husband.

The Holy Bible teaches that if you are arguing with a RATS or Crazy-Maker, you and the RATS or Crazy-Maker need to grow spiritually.

You cannot force a RATS or Crazy-Maker to grow up or correct their behaviour. Also, you are not obligated to guide someone else's spiritual growth unless they are your child. If the RATS or Crazy-Maker are now physically adults, they must learn to raise themselves spiritually.

You have a duty to share the wisdom of the Holy Bible, but you do not have a duty to raise a RATS or Crazy-Maker who has rejected the teachings of the Holy Bible.

Arguing with a RATS or Crazy-Maker keeps your focus on Satan's division and distractions and makes it difficult to hear God's Voice. Arguing with them also distracts you from accomplishing your Kingdom Assignment. God gave everyone free will. God did not give anyone the right to override anyone else's free will. The only exception is when the trespasser, such as a career criminal, has violated God's Commandments without remorse and intends to continue violating God's Commandments.

The only spirit you are allowed to change is your own. You need to grow spiritually and realize that arguing with the RATS or Crazy-Maker will not accomplish anything healthy.

You need to study Jesus as your role model and learn how to walk away, even if walking away is no more than a temporary timeout to prevent an escalation of conflict.

The truth is that there is no way of dealing with a RATS or Crazy-Maker; only God is strong enough to deal with them. If you are arguing with a RATS or Crazy-Maker, you will only force them to become more obstinate. They will entrench themselves more firmly into their gaslighting and passive-aggressive behaviour to protect their self-image from what they perceive as their gaslighting and passive-aggressive behaviour. RATSs and Crazy-Makers cannot conceive that you are actually attempting to help them; they see you as the same as themselves. Since they are already enemies to themselves, they also see you as enemies to their self-image. Since they cannot love themselves, they cannot comprehend how anyone else can love them.

If you are arguing with a RATS or Crazy-Maker, you do not have the right to control their behaviour, but you do have the right to walk away from harm. *If* you are arguing with a RATS or Crazy-Maker, *then* you are, in effect, transferring devils, demons, and other evil entities back and forth between you and your adversary. Each time the devils, demons, and other evil entities are transferred from one to another, they become stronger, and the conflict escalates.

> *Ecclesiastes 8:5-6 (KJV) Whoso keepeth the commandment shall feel no evil thing: and a wise man's heart discerneth both time and judgment. Because to every purpose there is time and judgment, therefore the misery of man is great upon him.*

The Holy Bible teaches that there is a proper time and place for everything and an appropriate manner to deal with a trespass.

If you believe that you are arguing with a RATS or Crazy-Maker, *then* I suggest that you ask God to help you comprehend the conflict from the perspective of the RATS or Crazy-Maker. If the conflict is based on the low self-esteem of the

RATS or Crazy-Maker, you now have a duty to protect or build up the spirit or self-esteem of the RATS or Crazy-Maker. This duty is the same as you would have for the immature spirit of your own son or daughter.

Remember that God loves all of his sons and daughters, including the RATS or Crazy-Maker you are struggling with. Remember also that there is a difference between naturally feelings-based reactions and spiritually emotions-based responses. If you are the more mature spirit, you have a duty to avoid your gut reactions and to act like the more mature spirit, responding with more mature emotions.

If you are a healthy two-dimensional or Four-Dimensional STAR, the RATS or Crazy-Maker in your life cannot be your spiritual equal, in the same manner that a young son or daughter cannot be the equal of the father or mother. The RATS or Crazy-Maker in your life may be physically an adult, but they are a spiritual toddler, child, or teenager.

Romans 14: 1 & 12-13 (KJV) Him that is weak in the faith receive ye, but not to doubtful disputations. So then every one of us shall give account of himself to God. Let us not therefore judge one another any more: but judge this rather, that no man put a stumblingblock or an occasion to fall in his brother's way.

*Acts 20:35 (KJV) I have shewed you all things, how that so labouring **ye ought to support the weak**, and to remember the words of the Lord Jesus, how he said, It is more blessed to give than to receive. [Emphasis added]*

Matthew 11:29-30 (KJV) Take my yoke upon you, and learn of me; for I am meek and lowly in heart: and ye shall find rest unto your souls. For my yoke is easy, and my burden is light.

The stronger must help the weaker to develop a stronger relationship with God. Jesus is the only begotten son of God and is, therefore, stronger than any Christian. In Matthew 11:29-30, Jesus offers his strength to help weaker Christians develop a stronger relationship with God.

If you have the patience and spiritual strength, and *if* you choose to help the RATS or Crazy-Maker, *then* you will need God's Help to help them grow from a spiritual toddler, child, or teenager into a spiritually mature STAR. As with a physical child, the developing personality style needs a safe environment at every level under the Kingdom of Heaven STAR.

When the RATS or Crazy-Maker in your life is learning their missing STAR styles, they will be tempted by the dark side. Jesus is the perfect light to guide the RATS or Crazy-Maker to becoming a STAR. Without the help of the Godhead, you will likely lock down your emotions in order to protect yourself. Locking down your emotions is like a prison lockdown where nothing gets in or out. The pain and hurt cannot get out to be removed from your spirit. And God's Grace and love cannot get in to heal your spirit.

Because of my Relationship Personality Style, I find it challenging to walk away from disharmony without doing everything that I can to heal the relationship. Because of my Technical Personality Style, I find it challenging to walk away from a false accusation without vindicating my character.

I have found it best to calmly inform the RATS or Crazy-Maker that I am aware of their unpleasant behaviour and that their behaviour violates Kingdom Principles, then walk away before the RATS or Crazy-Maker can start any gaslighting or passive-aggressive behaviour. I walk away from the RATS or Crazy-Maker because they will attempt to escalate the conflict to maintain control of the outcome. This solution is simple, but it is not easy.

Be certain that their behaviour is indeed a violation of Kingdom Principles as taught in the Holy Bible, or you might learn that you are the RATS and that you are gaslighting.

Do not allow the RATS or Crazy-Maker to rewrite history by denying their trespass. Do not allow them to claim that they are good Christians and choose only to remember the good things. When they deny the incidents of their trespasses, they will not be prepared to correct the trespass behaviour in the future.

Walking away from a RATS or Crazy-Maker might be temporary, like a timeout. Remember that RATSs and Crazy-Makers are spiritual children even if they are in physically adult bodies. In parenting, we often need to give the child a timeout to consider their bad behaviour. In dealing with RATSs or Crazy-Makers, you cannot enforce a timeout, so you need to effectively establish a timeout by walking away.

Hebrews 10:35-36 (KJV) Cast not away therefore your confidence, which hath great recompence of reward. For ye have need of patience, that, after ye have done the will [desire] of God, ye might receive the promise. [Clarification terms added]

*Matthew 16:1-4 (KJV) **And there came to him the Pharisees and Sadduccees tempting**: and they asked him to shew them a sign from heaven. But he answered and said to them: When it is evening, you say, It will be fair weather, for the sky is red. And in the morning: To day there will be a storm, for the sky is red and lowering. You know then how to discern the face of the sky: and can you not know the signs of the times? **A wicked and adulterous generation seeketh after a sign: and a sign shall not be given it**, but the sign of Jonas the prophet. **And he left them, and went away**. [Emphasis added]*

The Holy Bible teaches that you need confidence and patience to receive God's Promises. The same is true when protecting yourself from RATSs and Crazy-Makers.

If you are dealing with a RATS or Crazy-Maker, and if it is a repeated trespass, and *if* you have attempted admonishing and rebuking them, *then* you must calmly inform them of the unpleasant pattern that you have observed, clarify the behaviour that you will respond with in order to protect yourself, and then calmly walk away.

Joshua 24:24-27 & Judges 2:11-16 (KJV) And the people said unto Joshua, The LORD our God will we serve, and his voice will we obey. So Joshua made a covenant with the people that day, and set them a statute and an ordinance in Shechem. **And Joshua wrote these words in the book of the law of God, and took a great stone**, *and set it up there under an oak, that was by the sanctuary of the LORD. And Joshua said unto all the people, Behold,* **this stone shall be a witness unto us; for it hath heard all the words of the LORD which he spake unto us: it shall be therefore a witness unto you, lest ye deny your God. And the children of Israel did evil in the sight of the LORD, and served Baalim:** *And they forsook the LORD God of their fathers, which brought them out of the land of Egypt, and followed other gods, of the gods of the people that were round about them, and bowed themselves unto them, and provoked the LORD to anger. And they forsook the LORD, and served Baal and Ashtaroth.* **And the anger of the LORD was hot against Israel, and he delivered them into the hands of spoilers that spoiled them, and he sold them into the hands of their enemies round about**, *so that they could not any longer stand before their enemies. Whithersoever they went out, the hand of the LORD was against them for evil, as the LORD had said, and as the LORD had sworn unto them: and they were greatly distressed.* **Nevertheless the LORD raised up judges, which delivered them out of the hand of those that spoiled them**. *[Emphasis added]*

In Joshua 24:24-27 & Judges 2:11-16, the Holy Bible explains how God deals with RATSs and Crazy-Makers. First, establish an agreement on the boundary, then enforce discipline for the breach of the agreement. God enforced the boundary that had been agreed upon but did not permanently walk away from the Israelites. God raised judges to deliver them out of their suffering.

With each repeated trespass, calmly inform the RATS or Crazy-Maker of the boundary trespass, and then calmly enforce the boundary. Remember that you cannot change their behaviour, and you cannot enforce a boundary that forces change on them. However, you can enforce a boundary that protects your spirit from their repeated trespass. In a later section, I explain an approach (D.E.S.K.) that I have found effective for calmly dealing with boundary trespasses. You can use the DESK approach to express yourself even if they refuse to participate.

Just as RATSs and Crazy-Makers will often misquote the Holy Bible, they will also misquote and twist your words around to fit their argument. You might say something totally neutral, and they will either add words, remove words or change your words so that your words are now derogatory against them.

I have found it beneficial to record my conversations with RATSs or Crazy-Makers. I let them know that I am recording the conversation as audio notes only. Courts employ Court Recorders, but they use the recordings for legal purposes.

Dealing with RATSs or Crazy-Makers often feels like dealing with enemies, and the Holy Bible has clear instructions on dealing with everyone, including enemies. One pattern that I have observed is that RATSs and Crazy-Makers will rip apart their immediate family members with physical, verbal, and other forms of abuse while being model Christians to people outside the home. This negative behaviour is directed only at their own family because the RATS or Crazy-Maker desperately fight to protect their fragile self-image; the truth behind their secrets is impossible to hide from family members. However, there is no need to defend their secrets from people outside of the immediate family because they are not even aware of the existence of the secret, let alone the truth behind it.

Adults who keep secrets establish a doorway, foothold, or entry point for Satan to work his harm against their spirit. Once attached, Satan will harm the spirits of everyone in their family and social circle. Secrets are like the grapes in a winepress; whatever is pressed down into secrets will eventually leak out, but secrets leak out like toxic waste.

If you have a long history of conflict with a RATS or Crazy-Maker, you should think twice before putting yourself into a position where you cannot walk away easily, such as a long car ride, vacation, or even a restaurant. It won't matter if you are the driver or a passenger; if a conflict arises, it will be complicated to walk away. The RATS or Crazy-Maker will be able to escalate the conflict more easily.

Because of my desire for *precision of language*, I make a distinction between the terms discipline and punishment. Discipline focuses on correcting the behaviour while saving the individual, whereas punishment simply expresses anger against the individual. Speaking a negative expression starting with "It" or "That" followed by a positive expression starting with "You" is an example of discipline. Discipline leaves the individual knowing they are loved even though their behaviour is unloved. Speaking a negative expression starting with "You" without explanation or opportunity for reconciliation is an example of punishment. Punishment leaves the individual with the knowledge that they are unloved. In a later section, I explain how to use the DESK System for Difficult Conversations and Conflict Resolution.

INTROVERTED
PEOPLE
TASK
EXTROVERTED

17. Quality Communication

You will always find the facts to support the truths you seek. Right feelings follow right messages. Wrong feelings follow wrong messages. Right messages follow right feelings. Wrong messages follow wrong feelings.

Albert Mehrabian's 7-38-55 Rule

Messages are influenced by more than words. According to Albert Mehrabian's 7-38-55 Rule of Personal Communication concerning feelings, words only account for 7% of the message, while the quality of the voice accounts for 38%, and body language accounts for 55% of the message.

When you become angry, your body naturally tenses. Your arms might cross over your chest, and your hands might clench into fists. By deliberately changing your body language and controlling the quality of your voice, you can change the delivery of your message.

You do not experience the words; you experience the behaviour. When the words and the behaviour do not match, you must examine the behaviour to determine the truth. The truth is in the behaviour, and you can determine the truth by examining the patterns of behaviour.

Active Listening

There are many types of listening, and many people will distinguish between active, reflective, empathic, pleasure, learning, and investigative listening. For my purposes, Active Listening incorporates both reflective and empathic listening.

Active listening is a technique that requires the listener to fully concentrate, comprehend empathically, and respond appropriately without blame or judgment. It is impossible to fully concentrate if you are thinking about what you will say as soon as you have the opportunity to speak.

I admit that when I am doing my best to listen actively, I need to turn off my secondary Technical Personality Style to prevent myself from thinking about how I will respond; otherwise, I will stop listening and start thinking about my response.

Concentrate one hundred percent on the words, body language, and the style of the speaker's statements. Concentrating on the style means listening for expressions of details (task-oriented) or feelings (people-oriented); does the quality of voice reflect introversion or extroversion? With these three observations, it is possible to determine the speaker's personality style.

Ask for more details to ensure that you have all the details. Ask how the speaker feels. Act like a very gentle and compassionate investigator to ensure that you have all the details and all the feelings, and then ask the speaker for suggested solutions before considering what has been spoken. Asking for more information about their feelings will further help to determine their personality style.

Comprehend empathically by focusing on the feelings of the speaker. Empathy is more than Sympathy. Empathy requires your effort to really comprehend the other's feelings to the point of feeling their joy or pain. Sympathy is more like a superficial expression of happiness or sorrow in reflection of their feelings.

An example of Sympathy is: "I am sorry that you are experiencing emotional pain." An example of Empathy is: "I feel your suffering, and I feel like crying with you."

Respond appropriately and without blame or judgment. This pattern of response means first to reflect the details and emotions of the speaker and then to respond in their personality style.

If you are listening to someone with a Support Personality Style, there will be very little about details (other than possibly the goal). They will not want you to inject any details into the conversation; they only want to know how they can help complete the task at hand.

If you are listening to someone with a Technical Personality Style, there will be very little said about feelings (other than the frustration of a poorly executed process). They will not want you to inject any feelings into the conversation; they only want to know the steps you will take to complete the task at hand.

If you are listening to someone with an Action Personality Style, there will be very little about feelings (other than anger that the task is not completed). They will not want you to inject any feelings into the conversation; they only want to know that the task will be completed.

If you are listening to someone who has a Relationship Personality Style, there will be very few details (other than the names of the team working toward the goal). They will not want you to inject any details into the conversation; they only want to know how the team can work together in harmony to complete the task at hand.

Flattery Versus Edification

Edification is an Old English term meaning Compliment and/or Praise.

I have heard an expression: "Flattery will get you everywhere with me." The Holy Bible teaches that flattery is evil and praise is what we should look for in relationships.

Flattery

Webster's 1828 Dictionary defines flattery as "**False** praise; commendation bestowed for the purpose of gaining favor and influence, or to accomplish some purpose." [Emphasis added]

*Psalm 12:1-8 (KJV) Help, LORD; for the godly man ceaseth; for the faithful fail from among the children of men. **They speak vanity every one with his neighbour: with flattering lips and with a double heart do they speak. The LORD shall cut off all flattering lips, and the tongue that speaketh proud things**: Who have said, With our tongue will* *we prevail; our lips are our own: who is lord over us? For the oppression of the poor, for the sighing of the needy, now will I arise, saith the LORD; I will set him in safety from him that puffeth at him. The words of the LORD are pure words: as silver tried in a furnace of earth, purified seven times. Thou shalt keep them, O LORD, thou shalt preserve them from this generation for ever. The wicked walk on every side, when the vilest men are exalted. [Emphasis added]*

Daniel 11:32 (KJV) **And such as do wickedly against the covenant shall he corrupt by flatteries**: *but the people that do know their God shall be strong, and do exploits. [Emphasis added]*

Psalm 12 describes flattery as a tool the 'wicked' (RATSs) use to oppress the righteous (STARs). Daniel 11:32-40 explains that by using flattery, leaders will win over the population of non-believers and begin a greedy reign. Type 'Daniel 11:32-40' into any internet browser search engine to read all of the verses of Daniel 11:32-40.

Flattery is usually non-specific and untimely. When your RATS alarms are blaring, and you stand your ground as a STAR, the RATS will offer empty flattery such as "You are so smart" or "You are so wonderful," along with other seemingly nice words that you wished they had offered when you had actually done something worthy of praise.

If you challenge the RATS to give an example of how you were so smart or wonderful, they will be unable to recall any details because their flattery is empty, phoney, and fake.

Compliment

Webster's 1828 Dictionary defines Compliment as "an expression of civility, respect or regard, or to congratulate, as, to compliment a prince on the birth of a son."

Because of my desire for *precision of language*, I further define compliment as kind words focused on observable external accomplishments or actions rather than the character of the recipient.

The Holy Bible teaches that people will follow their naturally unkind ways without Holy Scripture. Society generally appears to be very negative. People always seek something to criticize and complain about some substandard service, so I try to spread encouragement and humour. Everyone makes occasional mistakes. If service has been mistakenly compromised, we should patiently help people recover and heal from their mistakes.

When shopping, I always look for some event or behaviour that I can complement. I always try to smile, tell a joke, and end the transaction with a happy farewell message.

One day, while at a baseball game, I was in line to buy a small lunch; a woman in front of me had styled her afro with braid extensions of blue and yellow, and I complimented her long, colourful braids.

She gave me a bright smile and a happy "Thank you. It is a lot of work to keep these braids looking good."

We exchanged a few more sentences, and we both parted, happier for the exchange.

When I am among friends, I will sometimes present a self-deprecating wit to get a laugh. The only place that I have not been able to get a smile reaction is in government buildings such as courthouses, licence renewal offices, etc. It seems that government personnel have special anti-smile training, or maybe they face so many unhappy customers that they have rewired the neurons of their brains to expect everyone to be an unhappy customer.

The concept of corporate culture suggests that the mood of the leaders of corporations affects the mood of the people working for the corporations. The worker's mood affects the customers' mood.

Praise

Webster's 1828 Dictionary defines Praise as "a Commendation bestowed on a person for his personal virtues or worthy actions, on meritorious actions themselves, or on anything valuable."

Because of my desire for *precision of language*, I further define praise as kind words focused on the perceived internal quality of character of the recipient rather than the observable accomplishment or actions.

Society generally appears to be very negative. People always seem to look for faults to complain about, as if every company and every individual intentionally cheats on every customer.

In addition to giving compliments with a smile, I am always looking for something that I can praise about the people who regularly take care of my shopping experience. As a result, I often get consistently excellent service.

One day, I entered the end of a long line just as an angry customer finished shouting at the woman behind the cash register. The woman looked like she would like to run away and cry. I have been on the receiving end of many similar angry outbursts in my lifetime. As the man stomped away, it was clear to me that there was nothing I could do to bring him peace, so I quietly waited in line. The woman behind the cash register had taken care of me in the past, so I knew that her service was consistently high quality. I gave her plenty of compliments and praise. By the time I left, she was smiling and thanked me for repairing her day.

I cannot guarantee that the quality of service that I receive at all the stores where I regularly shop is consistently high because of my habit of giving lots of compliments and praise. However, I would like to believe that I receive consistently high-quality service because people feel happier after serving me.

Compliment versus Praise

The difference between Compliment and Praise is slight. Generally, a compliment is given for an event or action completed, whereas praise pertains to an individual's character.

For example, it would be a compliment to say, "The chef has prepared a great meal." It would be praise to say, "The chef is truly skilled and always ensures to make every meal tasty."

Matthew 25:20-21 (KJV) And so he that had received five talents came and brought other five talents, saying, Lord, thou deliveredst unto me five talents: behold, I have gained beside them five talents more. His lord said unto him, Well done, thou good and faithful servant: thou hast been faithful over a few things, I will make thee ruler over many things: enter thou into the joy of thy lord.

Matthew 16:18 (KJV) And I say also unto thee, That thou art Peter, and upon this rock I will build my church; and the gates of hell shall not prevail against it.

Though the Holy Bible does not actually contain the word compliment, we are instructed to express words of edification to build people up and never to tear them down. In Matthew 25:21, Jesus gives us an example of a compliment for the servant's achievement of a profitable gain. In Matthew 16:18, Jesus praises Simon's character by surnaming him Peter, which is derived from the Greek word for rock.

Both compliments and praise should be specific and timely. *If* compliments and praise are only given during an argument, *then* the words are actually flattery and intended only for the speaker's gain.

If you cannot give eighty to ninety percent praise, compliments, and other forms of positive communication when you are around someone, *then* you might need to walk away. *If* you do not receive eighty to ninety percent praise, compliments, and other forms of positive communication when you are around someone, *then* you might need to walk away.

The Four Horsemen

John Gottman talks about the four horsemen of the marriage apocalypse. I have not studied John Gottman's teachings beyond hearing the list of the four horsemen in a casual conversation. However, the possible correlation between the horsemen and STAR Personality Styles is intriguing.

When I explain my version of the four horsemen of communication breakdown, I like to clarify that the pattern always starts with a disagreement as the catalyst.

1. Criticism: the defiant expression of pride
   a. These individuals use details to argue their positions. This pattern seems to resemble someone who is a Technical RATS.
2. Defensiveness: the passive expression of pride
   a. These individuals will retreat to find others who can help them and who appreciate their help. This pattern seems to resemble someone who is a Support RATS.
3. Contempt: the opposite of Respect – belittling sarcasm
   a. These individuals use results (or lack thereof) to argue their positions. This pattern seems to resemble someone who is an Action RATS.
4. Stonewalling: the silent treatment – hard-hearted
   a. These individuals use feelings to argue their positions. This pattern seems to resemble someone who is a negative Technical RATS.

Further to my correlation between the four horsemen and STAR Personality Styles, I believe that there is also a common pattern to most communication breakdowns. Criticism produces defensiveness, which in turn produces Contempt, which in turn produces Stonewalling.

Being quick to speak and slow to listen can present itself as criticism, ultimately leading to a breakdown in communication.

Criticism

Webster's 1828 Dictionary defines Criticism as "…The act of judging on the *merit* of a performance."

Because of my desire for *precision of language*, I take this a little farther for my own comprehension: Criticism means simultaneously blaming and judging a listener's lack of accomplishment. The critic presents a double whammy to the listener, keeping the focus away from the quality of the effort and keeping the focus on the judgment of the quality of the faulty result.

Criticism is similar to a complaint. Criticism is unkind words focused on observable accomplishments or actions rather than the character of the recipient. Complaint is unkind words focused on the perceived quality of the character of the recipient rather than the observable accomplishments or actions.

Why Questions

Questions that begin with "Why" reflect the perceptions and presumptions of the speaker.

> *Exodus 1:15-20 (KJV) And **the king of Egypt spake to the Hebrew midwives**, of which the name of the one was Shiphrah, and the name of the other Puah: And he said, When ye do the office of a midwife to the Hebrew women, and see them upon the stools; **if it be a son, then ye shall kill him**: but if it be a daughter, then she shall live. But the midwives feared God, and did not as the king of Egypt commanded them, but saved the men children alive. And the king of Egypt called for the midwives, and said unto them, **<u>Why</u> have ye done this thing, and have saved the men children alive**? And the midwives said unto Pharaoh, Because the Hebrew women are not as the Egyptian women; for they are lively, and are delivered ere the midwives come in unto them. Therefore God dealt well with the midwives: and the people multiplied, and waxed very mighty. [Emphasis added]*

In this Holy Scripture example, the *why question* reflected the truth. However, since *why questions* reflect the perceptions and presumptions of the speaker, starting any question with the word "Why" will often be interpreted as criticism. The word "Why" implies both a disagreement and a foregone conclusion of the true facts supporting your accusation against your opponent.

For example, consider this *why question*. "Why did you kill your neighbour?" This *why question* implies that the questioner disagrees with your decision to kill your neighbour, the questioner has evidence against you, and the questioner has already judged you as guilty of killing your neighbour.

Defensiveness

Webster's 1828 Dictionary defines Defensive as "... resisting attack or aggression; as defensive war, in distinction from offensive war, which is aggressive."

Again, because of my desire for *precision of language* I like to take this a little farther for my own comprehension. Defensiveness means simultaneously returning to blaming and judging a critic's unpleasant character. The speaker presents a double whammy to the critic, keeping the focus away from the quality of the result and keeping the focus on the judgment of the faulty character of the critic.

I believe that John Gottman's Criticism and Defensiveness are two sides of the same coin, and both are the product of the sin of pride.

Contempt

Webster's 1828 Dictionary defines Contempt as "The act of despising; the act of viewing or considering and treating as mean, vile and worthless; disdain; hatred of what is mean or deemed vile. This word is one of the strongest expressions of a mean opinion which the language affords."

The trespasser who emotes contempt has judged the sufferer as incompetent and undeserving of any redemption effort. Feelings don't matter. The process doesn't matter. Intent doesn't matter. Results are the only consideration.

Stonewalling

Webster's 1828 Dictionary definition of Stone-wall gives an image of what Stonewalling means: "A wall built of stones."

The sufferer has built a spiritual fortress around their heart, which is as impenetrable as a physical fortress.

Communication is like Driving on Ontario Roads

If the individuals have successfully advanced to the Two-Dimensional STAR stage, they already know their weaknesses and don't need others to emphasize their faults.

If you have never driven on highways in Ontario (Canada), *then* I must clarify two points before proceeding with the following few examples.

The first point to keep in mind is that drivers must drive on the right-hand side of a two-way street; this is relevant for scenario three. The second point to keep in mind: at the time of writing this book, Ontario drivers have No-Fault-Insurance, which means even if you are at fault, your insurance company still doesn't have to pay for damages and medical bills for the other driver(s) included in the accident.

This no-fault insurance information is not intended as legal advice, and there is no guarantee of accuracy. It is used only as an illustration about communication.

Scenario One:

This traffic accident example is oversimplified to focus on communication as it relates to personality styles.

Imagine a traffic accident where one driver is task-oriented, meaning that the details and process of the task are important, but feelings and emotions are not important. Imagine that the other driver is people-oriented, meaning that the feelings and emotions of the people are important, but the details and process are not important. In this example, I deliberately use opposing task-orientation and people-orientation to accentuate the communication breakdown. However, the breakdown would probably result in the same pattern regardless of orientation.

When a traffic accident occurs, task-oriented drivers tend to be quick to judge, especially if they also have a negative personality style. The Technical RATS knows exactly how things should be done correctly and quickly points out that you did something wrong. The Action RATS knows that the traffic accident has prevented them from reaching their destination; therefore, it must be your fault.

If the first driver to speak is a negative task-oriented RATS (Action or Technical), and *if* the other driver is people-oriented (Relationship or Support), *then* the people-oriented driver will be offended by the immediate judgment and rudeness of the task-oriented driver. The people-oriented driver will immediately react with people-oriented emotional defensiveness, especially if they have a negative people-oriented personality style.

Any negative expression can escalate the disagreement to conflict and conflict will drive the communication through the stages of the *four horsemen*. Nagging the drivers about their personality style weaknesses will probably be interpreted as *criticism* and only cause them to react with *defensiveness,* which will, in turn, escalate the conflict into *contempt*.

If the conflict is not resolved, it can escalate to contempt, especially if there is a perceived driver error <u>and</u> negative feelings have been displayed. The task-oriented driver's contempt for the emotional display of the people-oriented driver will cause the people-oriented driver to *stonewall*.

Once the conflict has devolved from contempt to stonewalling, a judge will need to settle the issue in traffic court.

This pattern of communication breakdown is especially true if there is a perceived driver error (task-oriented) <u>and</u> negative feelings have been displayed (people-oriented).

Scenario Two:

This traffic accident example is oversimplified to focus on communication as it relates to personality styles.

Let's imagine that a Technical Personality Style driver is driving eastbound on Highway 401, and there is no barrier between the eastbound and westbound lanes. Imagine that a Relationship Personality Style driver crosses over and collides with the *eastbound technical* driver. The *westbound relationship* driver is more to blame, if not one hundred percent to blame, for the collision.

Task-oriented personality styles tend to be quicker to judge. Suppose the *technical* driver argues with the *relationship* driver about blame due to driver error (task-oriented). In that case, the argument will not change the damage caused nor change the insurance claim process.

Suppose the *relationship* driver attempts to restore harmony (people-oriented) by explaining their distraction. In that case, the explanation will not change the damage caused nor change the insurance claim process.

If the *technical* driver started to argue with the *relationship* driver about blame, it might be perceived as a personal attack. It will probably cause an unnecessary escalation of conflict. If the *relationship* driver attempts to explain the cause of distraction, it might be perceived as an attempt to avoid blame and might cause an unnecessary escalation of conflict.

If the *technical* driver started shouting obscenities or throwing punches, the *relationship* driver could not be blamed for the violence; the *relationship* driver may have caused the accident; however, the *technical* driver caused the fight.

The next step should be to assess the damage to you and your property and to determine how to get you back on track to your destination. Getting back on track might require visiting an auto-body shop or a dealership to purchase a new car.

Scenario Three:

Let's consider another hypothetical collision, and please forgive the stereotypes in this example. A Technical Personality Style man is driving eastbound on a busy city street. A Relationship Personality Style woman is driving westbound. The man is very late for an important meeting and focused only on arriving on time (task-oriented). The woman is glancing at her makeup in the rear-view mirror while driving.

At a particular intersection, the *technical* driver needs to make a left-hand turn and makes the turn directly in front of the *relationship* driver. And a collision occurs.

The *technical* driver is definitely more to blame for the collision. The *relationship* driver was checking her makeup, but the *technical* driver failed to give her the right of way. Both drivers share a portion of the blame.

Arguing with the *relationship* driver about blame will not change the damage caused nor change the insurance-claim process. The *technical* driver's attempts to explain his rush will not change the damage caused nor change the insurance-claim process.

If the *relationship* driver started to argue with the *technical* driver about blame due to failure to give the right of way, *then* it might be perceived as a personal attack and probably result in unnecessary escalation to conflict.

If the technical driver started to argue with the relationship driver about blame due to her distraction, *then* it might be perceived as an attempt to avoid blame, and it might cause an unnecessary escalation of conflict.

The next step should be to assess the damage to you and your property and determine how to get you back on track to your destination. Getting back on track to your destination might require visiting an auto body shop or a dealership to purchase a new car.

Scenario Four:

Imagine a husband and wife, conveniently named Husband and Wife, who have a seemingly wonderful marriage. However, there is an old family secret that Husband's great-grandfather had an affair, resulting in illegitimate relatives.

Now imagine Husband who has a generational curse from his great-grandfather producing sexually promiscuous temptations and has an affair with his younger and very attractive co-worker. Husband is definitely more to blame, if not one hundred percent to blame, for the extra-marital affair. Arguing with Husband about blame will not change the damage caused by the affair, nor will it change the healing process. Any of Husband's attempts to explain the reason for his indiscretion will not change the damage caused by the affair, nor will it change the healing process.

If Wife starts to argue with Husband about blame, it might be perceived as a personal attack, and she will probably cause an unnecessary escalation of conflict. If Husband attempts to explain the cause of indiscretion, it might be perceived as an attempt to avoid blame and thereby cause an unnecessary escalation of conflict.

The next step should be to assess the damage to you and your marriage and determine how to get you back on track to your destination. Getting back on track to your destination might require visiting a marriage counsellor or searching for a new marriage if reconciliation is not possible.

Summary:

In general, relationship conflict is quite similar to the collision examples. Assigning blame or determining the cause of the trespass is not as important as assessing the damage of the trespass and determining how to get back on track to your destination.

In the driving examples, getting back on track to your destination might require visiting an auto body shop or the dealership to purchase a new car.

In this conflict situation, getting back on track to your destination might require visiting a marriage counsellor or searching for a new marriage if reconciliation is not possible.

Genesis 2:7 (KJV) And the LORD God formed man of the dust of the ground, and breathed into his nostrils the breath of life; and man became a living soul.

Genesis 2:15-18 (KJV) And the LORD God took the man, and put him into the garden of Eden to dress it and to keep it. And the LORD God commanded the man, saying, Of every tree of the garden thou mayest freely eat: But of the tree of the knowledge of good and evil, thou shalt not eat of it: for in the day that thou eatest thereof thou shalt surely die. And the LORD God said, It is not good that the man should be alone; I will make him an help meet for him.

Genesis 2:21-22 (KJV) And the LORD God caused a deep sleep to fall upon Adam, and he slept: and he took one of his ribs, and closed up the flesh instead thereof; And the rib, which the LORD God had taken from man, made he a woman, and brought her unto the man.

Genesis 2:25 (KJV) And they were both naked, the man and his wife, and were not ashamed.

Genesis 3:1-7 (KJV) Now the serpent was more subtle than any beast of the field which the LORD God had made. And he said unto the woman, Yea, hath God said, Ye shall not eat of every tree of the garden? And the woman said unto the serpent, We may eat of the fruit of the trees of the garden: But of the fruit of the tree which is in the midst of the garden, God hath said, Ye shall not eat of it, neither shall ye touch it, lest ye die. And the serpent said unto the woman, Ye shall not surely die: For God doth know that in the day ye eat thereof, then your eyes shall be opened, and ye shall be as gods, knowing good and evil. And when the woman saw that the tree was good for food, and that it was pleasant to the eyes, and a tree to be desired to make one wise, she took of the fruit thereof, and did eat, and gave also unto her husband with her; and he did eat. And the eyes of them both were opened, and they knew that they were naked; and they sewed fig leaves together, and made themselves aprons.

God created a perfect environment for Adam and Eve. Evil pride came in and seduced them both to substitute God's Will with self-will, and sin and the generational curse of Original Sin entered into Man's World. It is important to note that they are equally guilty of the same sin. Adam was standing beside Eve and did nothing to stop her.

Personality Styles' and Messages

If you are listening to someone with a Support Personality Style, there will be very little about details (other than expressing the goal). They will not want you to inject any details into the conversation; they only want to know how they can help complete the task at hand.

If you are listening to someone with a Technical Personality Style, there will be very little about feelings (other than the frustration of a poorly executed process). They will not want you to inject any feelings into the conversation; they only want to know the steps you will take to complete the task at hand.

If you are listening to someone with an Action Personality Style, there will be very little about feelings (other than anger that the task is not completed). They will not want you to inject any feelings into the conversation; they only want to know that the task will be completed.

If you are listening to someone with a Relationship Personality Style, there will be very few details (other than the names of the team working toward the goal). They will not want you to inject any details into the conversation; they only want to know how the team can work together in harmony to complete the task at hand.

To use the STAR Personality Style system, listen for what is <u>not</u> spoken as well as what <u>is</u> spoken. Listen for words associated with feelings or emotions to determine if the speaker is people-oriented. Listen for words associated with procedures, rules, or goals to determine if the speaker is task-oriented. Pay attention to the speaker's body language, tone of voice, or 'quality of voice' in order to determine whether the speaker is extroverted or introverted. With these three observations, it is possible to determine the speaker's primary STAR personality style.

When you speak to someone, watch for their body language and their verbal responses to the personality style you are presenting. You can learn empathy by carefully and objectively observing their responses to your personality style. Listen for the metamessage (or patterns) in communications.

Personality Styles' Impact On Quality Messages:

People with Technical Personality Styles are basically task-oriented and typically very detail-oriented. They carefully consider facts before deciding on rules. This pattern can set them up to be quick to speak and slow to listen.

People with Action Personality Style individuals are basically task-oriented and typically very focused on results. This pattern can set them up to be quick to speak and slow to listen.

People with either a Relationship Personality Style or a Support Personality Style are basically people-oriented and typically very focused on feelings. This pattern can set them up to be quick to speak and slow to listen.

18. Conflict

Comprehension of any information or message is determined by content, relationship, and context. To explain this from the perspective of my Technical Personality Style, I would write: *Comprehension = Content + Relationship + Context.*

The nouns, which are the things in the message, are the *content* of the message. The verbs, which are the actions in the message, are the *relationship* of the message. The words surrounding the subject, which is the noun that is doing something, and the object, which is the noun that is receiving the action, are the *context* of the message.

To clarify the comprehension formula, consider this example. If a message contains a car and a driver as content, there can be no *comprehension* of the message until the relationship and context can be determined. The relationship of the message might be for sale, for repair, or involved in an accident.

If we combine the content of the 'damaged car' and the 'injured driver' with a relationship of 'involved in an accident,' we might assume that the driver was driving the car when it was involved in an accident.

However, *if* we add context that the injury occurred on a football field and that the accident occurred several months before while the car was parked, *then* we might now comprehend that another driver crashed into the injured driver's parked car, and the injured driver had difficulty getting in and out of the car due to the football injuries.

There can be no comprehension of the message without clarity between the content, relationship, and context. Our brains are designed to quickly evaluate facts and make a quick determination as a natural defence mechanism. If a baseball (content) is flying (relationship) towards your head (context), you should quickly raise your glove before the relationship and context change to hit you in the head.

18. Conflict

Our brains instantaneously perceive different factors to make a determination of a spoken message. Mistakes in comprehension often cause conflicts. According to Albert Mehrabian's 7-38-55 Rule of Personal Communication, words account for only seven percent of the message. Ninety-three percent of the message is related to the delivery of the message. Delivery is the context of the message and is impacted by the personality style of the receiver.

True conflict should always be internal and exist only because of tension between the natural and spiritual. Conflict should never be between the sufferer and the trespasser unless the trespasser is proven to be your enemy who intended to harm you.

The real conflict should always be _your_ natural body's feelings-based reaction and _your_ growing spirit's emotions-based response based on Kingdom Principles.

> *Romans 7:15 (KJV) For that which I do I allow not: for what I would, that do I not; but what I hate, that do I.*

In Romans 7:15, Paul explains that he had the same struggle between his nature and his spirit. This conflict between natural and spiritual has existed for approximately two thousand years since Paul wrote about it.

> *Luke 12:51-53 (KJV) Suppose ye that I am come to give peace on earth? I tell you, Nay; but rather division: For from henceforth there shall be five in one house divided, three against two, and two against three. The father shall be divided against the son, and the son against the father; the mother against the daughter, and the daughter against the mother; the mother in law against her daughter in law, and the daughter in law against her mother in law.*

Jesus did not come to eliminate conflict because conflict is necessary for spiritual growth. The Holy Bible teaches that Jesus' followers are guaranteed to experience conflict in the world since it does not adhere to Kingdom Principles. Just as a seed must be destroyed to make way for the seedling, relationships must undergo conflict to make way for spiritual growth.

There is always at least one trespasser (or transgressor) in every conflict, at least one trespass (or transgression), and at least one sufferer who either has been wronged or perceives that a wrong has been committed. It takes at least two people to have a conflict, and both are at least partially to blame. However, there is always one who is more to blame (the trespasser) than the other (the sufferer).

Unless the trespass was done deliberately, the trespasser might not be aware of the trespass. The outcome of the trespass is now up to the sufferer. *If* the sufferer reacts out of feelings of anger, resentment or bitterness, *then* conflict is born. *If* the sufferer pauses to consider the trespass through the trespasser's mind, heart, and will, led by the Holy Spirit, *then* the sufferer might first forgive and investigate further before responding with a spirit-led emotion.

The resolution requires at least two people, but unfortunately, it only takes one person to keep the conflict at an impasse. Usually, the trespasser's refusal to repent causes the impasse. However, the sufferer's refusal to forgive can also cause an impasse. *If* the trespasser used a negative personality style to trespass against the sufferer, *then* the trespasser must use the sufferer's positive personality style to atone and reconcile.

*Deuteronomy 5:9 (KJV) Thou shalt not bow down thyself unto them, nor serve them: for I the LORD thy God am a jealous God, visiting the **iniquity [secret sin]** of the fathers upon the children unto the third and fourth generation of them that hate me [wicked], [Emphasis and Clarification terms added]*

According to Webster's 1828 Dictionary:

- A transgression is an act of passing over or beyond any law or rule of moral duty; the violation of a law or known principle of rectitude; breach of command.

- A transgressor is one who breaks a law or violates a command; one who violates any known rule or principle of rectitude; a sinner.
- A trespass is to commit any offence or to do any act that injures or annoys another; to violate any rule of rectitude to the injury of another.
- A trespasser is one who commits a trespass. Literally, to pass beyond; hence primarily, to pass over the boundary line …
- A sufferer is one who endures or undergoes pain, either of body or spirit (mind, heart, or will), one who sustains inconvenience or loss, as suffers by poverty or sickness. A Sufferer can either accept or reject the offence.

Usually, I like to use Webster's 1828 Dictionary to interpret words in the Holy Bible. Sometimes, I prefer to allow the Holy Bible to interpret the words in the Holy Bible. Iniquity and wickedness are two words that I have determined my own definitions of based on content, relationship, and context found in various verses in the Holy Bible.

Iniquity is a transgression or trespass in which the transgressor or trespasser attempts to keep the action secret from everyone, including God.

Wickedness is a deliberate self-justification and repetition of transgressions or trespasses.

*Numbers 20:3, 6-13 (KJV) And **the people chode with Moses**, and spake, saying, Would God that we had died when our brethren died before the LORD! And Moses and Aaron went from the presence of the assembly unto the door of the tabernacle of the congregation, and they fell upon their faces: and the glory of the LORD appeared unto them. **And the LORD spake unto Moses**, saying, Take the rod, and gather thou the assembly together, thou, and Aaron thy brother, and **speak ye unto the rock** **before their eyes**; and it shall give forth his water, and thou shalt bring forth to them water out of the rock: so thou shalt give the congregation and their beasts drink. And Moses took the rod from before the LORD, as he commanded him. And Moses and Aaron gathered the* congregation together before the rock, and he said unto them, **Hear now, ye rebels**; must we fetch you water out of this rock? And **Moses lifted up his hand, and with his rod he smote the rock twice**: and the water came out abundantly, and the congregation drank, and their beasts also. And the LORD spake unto Moses and Aaron, Because ye believed me not, to sanctify me in the eyes of the children of Israel, therefore ye shall not bring this congregation into the land which I have given them. This is the water of Meribah; because the children of Israel strove with the LORD, and he was sanctified in them. [Emphasis added]

Leviticus 4:2-3 (KJV) Speak unto the children of Israel, saying, **If a soul shall sin through ignorance against any of the commandments of the LORD concerning things which ought not to be done**, and shall do against any of them: If the priest that is anointed do sin according to the sin of the people; **then let him bring for his sin**, which he hath sinned, a young bullock without blemish unto the LORD **for a sin offering**. [Emphasis added]

2 Kings 5:15-19 (KJV) And he returned to the man of God, he and all his company, and came, and stood before him: and he said, **Behold, now I know that there is no God in all the earth, but in Israel**: now therefore, I pray thee, take a blessing of thy servant. But he said, As the LORD liveth, before whom I stand, I will receive none. And he urged him to take it; but he refused. And Naaman said, Shall there not then, I pray thee, be given to thy servant two mules' burden of earth? for thy servant will henceforth offer neither burnt offering nor sacrifice unto other gods, but unto the LORD. **In this thing the LORD pardon thy servant, that when my master goeth into the house of Rimmon to worship there, and he leaneth on my hand, and I bow myself in the house of Rimmon: when I bow down myself in the house of Rimmon, the LORD pardon thy servant in this thing**. And he said unto him, Go in peace. So he departed from him a little way. [Emphasis added]

John 13:34-35 (KJV) A new commandment I give unto you, That ye love one another; as I have loved you, that ye also love one another. By this shall all men know that ye are my disciples, if ye have love one to another.

Iniquities, transgressions, trespasses, or wickedness are sins, but not all sins are iniquities, transgressions, trespasses, or wickedness.

Though I will often speak of sin generally instead of using the more specific categories, I believe *precision of language* sometimes improves comprehension. Sin is a catch-all term for any action contrary to God's Laws or Statutes.

Some sins result from reacting before thinking, which can sometimes be followed by immediate repentance, as in Numbers 20:3, 6-13. Other sins result from not knowing God's Laws, as in Leviticus 4:2-3. Still, other sins result from threat, duress, or intimidation, as in 2 Kings 5:15-19.

To satisfy my desire for *precision of language*, I have produced this definition for sin: Sin is any action that takes away from and does not enhance one's relationship with God or with one another, including animals, earth, etc.

Everyone has boundaries, whether they are aware of them or not. The problem in many conflicts might be one of two reasons. First, trespassers might not be aware of the trespass because sufferers are not protecting their boundaries. Second, transgressors might deliberately violate laws to trample boundaries and steal from the sufferers. It is the violation of the boundaries that causes pain, which in turn results in conflict.

> *Luke 17:1-4 (KJV) Then said he unto the disciples, It is impossible but that offences will come: but woe unto him, through whom they come! It were better for him that a millstone were hanged about his neck, and he cast into the sea, than that he should offend one of these little ones. Take heed to yourselves: If thy brother trespass against thee, rebuke him; and if he repent, forgive him. And if he trespass against thee seven times in a day, and seven times in a day turn again to thee, saying, I repent; thou shalt forgive him.*

I believe that disagreements are inevitable, but conflicts are avoidable. It is not a question of if there will be a disagreement but when.

Disagreements occur when we experience something that appears to be a trespass. Conflict results from escalated disagreements when we come to a decision or judgment without any flexibility, and a trespass has occurred.

When dealing with feelings, we must stop and spiritually evaluate the circumstances before responding with godly emotions. When we experience disagreements, we need to stop and spiritually consider the details of the experience to evaluate what really happened correctly. Whether in disagreement or conflict, the trespasser or transgressor who caused the suffering is guiltier, and it would be better for him to tie a millstone around his neck and be cast into the sea to cause the sufferer to sin.

After the transgression or trespass has occurred, the sin cannot be undone. The sufferer has two choices: either to commit a feeling-based reactive sin _or_ to forgive, consider the offence with their spirit and then respond with godly emotions. Forgiving does not mean forgetting or condoning the trespass. Atonement and/or reconciliation may still be required to restore trust after forgiveness.

Ephesians 4:26 (KJV) Be ye angry, and sin not: let not the sun go down upon your wrath:

In Ephesians 4:26, Paul warns us not to let the sun go down upon our wrath.

Ephesians 4:26 does <u>not</u> tell us that we must totally resolve all conflict issues before the sun goes down. It means that we need to resolve our negative participation in the conflict.

If we are the trespasser who initiated the conflict and we are aware of the trespass, *then* we must *repent* before the sun goes down. *If* we are the sufferer of the conflict and we are aware of the trespass, *then* we must *forgive* before the sun goes down.

Full atonement or restitution of the conflict might take time. Forgiveness is required immediately, but forgetting is not required until the trespasser has produced evidence of the fruits of repentance.

It is important to comprehend that <u>all</u> negative participation in conflict is a sin. Any argument, passive-aggression, defensiveness, or any other type of negative participation in any conflict is a win for Satan.

The trespasser might be unable to participate in healthy behaviour. The trespasser might believe that negative behaviour is better than no participation. Or they might be deliberately controlling to steal from the sufferer.

In parent-child relationships, some children might misbehave to fulfill their need for attention. Receiving punishment for bad behaviour might be considered better than no attention for good behaviour (some attention is better than no attention).

*1 Corinthians 3:18-19 (KJV) Let no man deceive himself. If any man among you seemeth to be **wise in this world**, let him become a fool, that he may be wise. For the wisdom of this world is foolishness with God. For it is written, He taketh the wise in their own craftiness. [Emphasis added]*

Without God, we cannot easily compete with someone who believes and proclaims himself to be wise.

The only peaceful solution for dealing with an adult RATS or Crazy-Maker is to walk away. Maybe you walk away only for a temporary timeout, with a reunion possible after one or both people grow towards becoming a Kingdom of Heaven STAR. Completing the journey to becoming a Kingdom of Heaven STAR might take an entire lifetime. It will be a lonely journey if not shared with another STAR.

We measure our fault based on our intentions. However, we assign the other's fault based on our observation and interpretation of their behaviour. Our interpretation of their behaviour might be clouded by our experience or by our own self-talk.

Matthew 18:15-18 (KJV) Moreover if thy brother shall trespass against thee, go and tell him his fault between thee and him alone: if he shall hear thee, thou hast gained thy brother. But if he will not hear thee, then take with thee one or two more, that in the mouth of two or three witnesses every word may be established. And if he shall neglect to hear them, tell it unto the church: but if he neglect to hear the church, let him be unto thee as an heathen man and a publican [tax collector]. Verily I say unto you, Whatsoever ye shall bind on earth shall be bound in heaven: and whatsoever ye shall loose on earth shall be loosed in heaven. [Clarification terms added]

Luke 3:8 (KJV) Bring forth therefore fruits worthy of repentance, ….

The Holy Bible gives us instructions on how to correctly deal with conflict through the Lord Jesus Christ's words.

Matthew 5:27-28 (KJV) Ye have heard that it was said by them of old time, Thou shalt not commit adultery: But I say unto you, That whosoever looketh on a woman to lust after her hath committed adultery with her already in his heart.

Jesus further explains that thinking about a sinful action and the actual commission of sin are equally sinful. Many verses in the Holy Bible instruct us to capture our thoughts so that the thoughts cannot lead us to the actual commission of sin.

An in-depth and honest study of the Holy Bible will provide plenty of information to satisfy each of the STAR Personality Styles: compassion and healing for the Support Style, correct thinking and rules for the Technical Style, repercussions for non-compliance of laws for the Action Style, harmony advice for the Relationship Style.

Without abandoning their own primary personality style, each personality style can improve social interactions through true compliance with all of the Biblical principles and teachings.

The Holy Bible explains the technical rules, rituals, and procedures for anyone who is a primary Technical STAR to achieve the love, peace, and harmony needed by anyone who is a primary Relationship STAR. Devils, demons, other evil entities and principalities, minions and nominees block this knowledge to achieve interpersonal chaos, allowing for easier control and profit.

Although very profitable for lawyers, judges, and others in the legal industry, it is unfortunate that children are not taught life skills, such as biblical principles, the power of positive thinking, conflict resolution, etc. Children should be taught at a young age when it is easier to rewire the child's brain. If boys and girls are taught godly principles at a young age, later legal issues could be significantly reduced. The court system is an adversarial process pitting people against each other. As courtroom conflict escalates, lawyers, judges, and everyone involved in the judicial system benefit.

Most politicians are educated as lawyers, and their focus appears to be more on courtroom drama than improving society. The legislative process seems to be as adversarial as courtrooms. Governments might benefit from a preponderance of psychotherapists being elected into office.

Matthew 23:23 (KJV) Woe unto you, scribes and Pharisees, hypocrites! for ye pay tithe of mint and anise and cummin, and have omitted the weightier matters of the law, judgment, mercy, and faith: these ought ye to have done, and not to leave the other undone.

Luke 11:46 (KJV) And he said, Woe unto you also, ye lawyers! for ye lade men with burdens grievous to be borne, and ye yourselves touch not the burdens with one of your fingers.

In the Holy Bible, Pharisees and scribes are the equivalents of today's lawyers, judges and politicians, and Jesus described them as hypocrites. Jesus was focused on reclaiming the people from the hypocrites, who unfairly labelled them as sinners, and redeeming their souls to God.

Satan promises the pleasure of revenge, but his pleasure is only temporary, especially if a devil has attached to the spirit of your opponent; the devil will trigger immediate retaliation.

Each time we submit to the temptation of revenge, it strengthens the devil.

If you are participating in aggression or other negative behaviour, you are never more than the weightlifter's spotter in Satan's transactions; you can almost feel the devil getting stronger while you only become increasingly bitter. When you deliberately trigger others, you open a door and invite demons into the mind, heart, and will of both you and your adversary. Once Satan's devils, demons, and other evil entities and principalities have a foothold or an attachment has been established, it becomes more difficult to remove Satan's attachment to them.

Strife never improves your quality of life, social interactions, or relationships. Instead, strife will always deteriorate your joy in life, social interactions, and relationships. We waste so much energy dealing with strife when the true challenge is becoming the best spiritual being that we can be.

Walking away from the strife is not the same as permanently walking away from the relationship. If you are a more advanced STAR than your partner, you might need to walk away temporarily as a timeout. Just as teenagers need space and time to grow independently, your spiritually less mature RATS or Crazy-Maker needs time and space to grow independently.

If the less advanced partner refuses to grow up, *then* you should ask yourself, "What Would Jesus Do?". You might need to walk away permanently to protect yourself from being dragged back to a lower level of negative personality style. I highly recommend reading "When to Walk Away" by Pastor Gary Thomas so that you know when to walk away temporarily and when to walk away permanently.

If you are most frequently the trespasser in your conflicts, *then* you should self-impose a zero-tolerance policy for your offending behaviour. Once you have decided that a zero-tolerance policy is necessary, you must stop all internal debates on the topic of your temptation. You must eliminate all images, thoughts, words, actions and non-actions that will bring you into the circle of temptation.

Regarding relationships, a zero-tolerance policy is not about eliminating fun from your life. Unhealthy relationships can only give temporary pleasure. A zero-tolerance policy is about learning to establish and enjoy the best that healthy relationships can permanently bring into your life.

Five Stages of Grief

Life has a one hundred percent mortality rate. There is only one way to get out of life, and that is death.

I will be the first to admit that I am not an expert in Elizabeth Kubler-Ross' theory of the five stages of grief: denial, anger, bargaining, depression, and finally, acceptance.

I have not studied Elizabeth Kubler-Ross' theory of the five stages of grief beyond a casual conversation while sharing biblical wisdom and how it seemed to apply in my own life. However, the possible correlation between Elizabeth Kubler-Ross' theory of the five stages of grief and STAR Personality Styles is intriguing.

Some of the objections I have heard are that not everyone will go through all five stages before death, some might regress through the stages, and some will bypass some of the stages. Not everyone will actually make it to the acceptance stage before death.

Stage 1 is denial, focusing on the process and facts. Somewhere in the process or facts, there was an error. This stage seems to be task-oriented and very much like the Technical Personality Style.

Stage 2 is anger, and the focus is on the inability to avoid the inevitable death and failure to accomplish a goal of life. This stage seems to be task-oriented and very much like the Action Personality Style.

Stage 3 is bargaining, which focuses on changing habits to earn the right to continue with life; usually, the bargaining is with God. This stage seems to be people-oriented and very much like the Relationship Personality Style.

Stage 4 is depression, and the focus is on worrying about caring for people left behind and how to make amends for trespasses that have not been righted. This stage seems to be people-oriented and very much like the Support Personality Style.

Stage 5 is acceptance, and the focus is on peaceful acceptance of the inevitable with no way to change the outcome; this is not the same as acceptance that the unavoidable is okay. This stage seems to be the culmination of all the personality styles – the Four-Dimensional or Kingdom of Heaven STAR.

In my divorce experience, the order of the stages was bargaining, denial, depression, acceptance, and anger. In the bargaining stage, my bargaining was primarily with God but also with my ex-wife. Anger did not set in until I had experienced the one-dimensional thinking of the gender prejudice, gender injustice, and inequality of the Family Court system.

My ex-wife was addicted to spending and gambling, and she left me a few weeks after I separated our bank accounts and told her that I would no longer bail out her spending or gambling losses. I had told her I would continue to pay for all reasonable family expenses and that she could only spend the money she earned as a divorce lawyer's assistant.

Luke 11:11-13 (KJV) If a son shall ask bread of any of you that is a father, will he give him a stone? or if he ask a fish, will he for a fish give him a serpent? Or if he shall ask an egg, will he offer him a scorpion? If ye then, being evil, know how to give good gifts unto your children: how much more shall your heavenly Father give the Holy Spirit to them that ask him?

We know from the Holy Bible that God's Love is unconditional even when we sin or reject God.

God loves us even when we choose to follow Satan and sin against God or even reject God. I know the truth about God's Love because I am a father, and God's Ability to love is much more powerful than mine. I love all of my children even though I have not seen my oldest two children since January 2004.

I was angry with God for the first three years after my wife left me. This duration is how long it took for me to realize that God did not cause my divorce and that my ex-wife had used her free will to take revenge against me for protecting my family's finances from her addictions. God used the tribulation of my divorce to grow me into becoming a better man. I remained angry with my ex-wife throughout the eleven years that she dragged me into the gender-prejudiced Family Court.

Today, I no longer hold any anger or bitterness against my wife for the tribulation of the divorce. Forgiveness and the Holy Spirit helped me to see the true root of the harm. My ex-wife could not have harmed me were it not for the systemic injustice of gender prejudice, gender injustice, and gender inequality in the Family Court system. All of the harm done to me was done with the full knowledge, permission, and assistance of the Family Court system. Forgiving my ex-wife was possible only after I realized that the gender-prejudiced Family Court, and not my ex-wife, is the true root of the harm. My most painful loss was the loss of my time with my children; possibly, my children will read this book and find a way to reconnect with me.

Not all relationships are between people. We also have relationships with the legal system. Here are two lessons that I learned that could benefit any man whose wife has asked him for a divorce. *First,* do not initiate divorce proceedings or acquiesce to your wife's divorce demands to initiate the divorce proceedings, even if your wife promises to let you see your children without interference. Initiating the divorce, as the 'Applicant,' tells the prejudicial family court that <u>you</u> (the man) abandoned your family.

Second, do not allow lawyers to convince you that "irreconcilable differences" is an acceptable reason for divorce. Claiming Irreconcilable differences makes it easy for the lawyers. However, the relationship rules of the Holy Bible require the husband to be responsible for his ex-wife for the rest of his days. This biblical duty is explained further in the Grounds for Divorce in the later section of Relationship Rules of the Holy Bible.

Genesis 50:15-21 (KJV) And when Joseph's brethren saw that their father was dead, they said, Joseph will peradventure hate us, and will certainly requite us all the evil which we did unto him. And they sent a messenger unto Joseph, saying, Thy father did command before he died, saying, So shall ye say unto Joseph, Forgive, I pray thee now, the trespass of thy brethren, and their sin; for they did unto thee evil: and now, we pray thee, forgive the trespass of the servants of the God of thy father. And Joseph wept when they spake unto him. And his brethren also went and fell down before his face; and they said, Behold, we be thy servants. And Joseph said unto them, Fear not: for am I in the place of God? But as for you, ye thought evil against me; but God meant it unto good, to bring to pass, as it is this day, to save much people alive. Now therefore fear ye not: I will nourish you, and your little ones. And he comforted them, and spake kindly unto them.

Romans 8:28 (KJV) And we know that all things work together for good to them that love God, to them who are the called according to his purpose.

I do not share my experiences to persecute anyone or to attract sympathy. The Holy Bible teaches that God can turn evil intentions and actions into something beneficial. My tribulation with the Family Law court was according to God's Plan.

We are the sum-total of every lesson that we have experienced. I like who I am today, so I look back on my trials and tribulations with gratitude for God's Help to overcome them and for the spiritual growth that I experienced.

Still, I pray that I never need to repeat the tribulation of divorce.

I would not be the man I am today were it not for the trials and tribulations that the Holy Spirit has helped me overcome. I pray (almost every day) for the forgiveness and salvation of many people, and my ex-wife and my first two children are included in my prayers.

> *Luke 22:39-44 (KJV) And he came out, and went, as he was wont, to the mount of Olives; and his disciples also followed him. And when he was at the place, he said unto them, Pray that ye enter not into temptation. And he was withdrawn from them about a stone's cast, and kneeled down, and prayed, Saying, Father, if thou be willing, remove this cup from me: nevertheless not my will, but thine, be done. And there appeared an angel unto him from heaven, strengthening him. And being in an agony he prayed more earnestly: and his sweat was as it were great drops of blood falling down to the ground.*

Luke 22:39-44 teaches that Jesus displayed depression, bargaining, and finally acceptance, but did <u>not</u> display anger.

Fight, Flight, Freeze, Or Fix

The term fight-or-flight response is common, but I would like to add a couple of new words to the mix about conflict within the context of marriage. The *fight* response is obviously an argument; this could possibly pertain to the Action Personality Style. The *flight* response is akin to getting a divorce; this could possibly pertain to the Technical Personality Style. The *freeze* response would probably put the relationship into deep freeze by starting an adulterous affair or stonewalling; this could possibly pertain to Relationship or Support Personality Styles. The *fix* response is only possible when the people in conflict grow and become at least a Four-Dimensional or Kingdom of Heaven STAR.

Two Ears, Two Eyes, and One Mouth

You have two ears, two eyes, and only one mouth, so you should watch and listen twice as much as you speak. Use your two eyes to observe; use your two ears to listen; together, your eyes and ears will allow you to study the experience and determine the true facts to present to your mind and heart in order to express your will by responding with a godly response.

Pastor Andy Stanley recommends that you quickly unclench your hands while you quietly say the phrase "Quick to Listen and Slow to Speak" in your mind. By practicing the phrase and unclenching your hands while thinking calm, peaceful thoughts, you will establish an anchor that can help you to remain calm in times of conflict.

*Philippians 2:3-5 (KJV) Let nothing be done through strife or vainglory; but in lowliness of mind let each esteem other better than themselves. **Look** not every man on his own things, but every man also on the things of others. Let this mind be in you, which was also in Christ Jesus: [Emphasis added]*

*Proverbs 18:15 (KJV) The heart of the prudent getteth knowledge; and the **ear** of the wise seeketh knowledge. [Emphasis added]*

*Proverbs 24:32 (KJV) Then I saw, and **considered it well**: I looked upon it, and **received instruction**. [Emphasis added]*

Before taking any action against anyone, it is important to study the trespasser to determine the truth. The Holy Bible teaches that we should look and listen and then consider the facts to receive spiritual instruction on the proper emotional response.

Before you speak against a trespasser, pray for God's Help to comprehend the trespasser's thoughts and motivation. With your eyes, look for observable behaviours. With your ears, listen for personality styles and needs.

In keeping with Pastor Andy Stanley's strategy for being quick to listen and slow to speak, you should encourage the speaker to speak more by asking open-ended questions, such as who, what, when, where and how. Avoid asking Why questions because they can initiate or escalate conflict.

Words are powerful. According to Pastor Andy Stanley, words are not equally weighted. Depending on the message, the sender, and the amount of time needed to heal, it can take more than ten positive messages to erase one negative message. No negative messages can be healed immediately; they all require time to heal. Emotionally charged or hurtful messages, especially from significant others, will be remembered for a long time and possibly for a lifetime.

> Negative messages from bosses produce more damage than negative messages from coworkers.
> Negative messages from moms produce more damage than negative messages from bosses.
> Negative messages from dads produce more damage than negative messages from moms.
> Negative messages from sons and daughters produce more damage than negative messages from people outside the immediate family (*biological* family of origin).

I have many favourite books in the Holy Bible, and the book of James is high on that list. James was the brother of Jesus, born to Mary and Joseph. James was not a follower of Jesus until James saw and spoke to Jesus after Jesus died, was buried, and was raised from the dead by God. The Holy Bible teaches that becoming sealed in the Book of Life and getting into the Kingdom of Heaven is as simple as honestly and sincerely declaring this Christian truth.

However, it is not easy to be a True Christian. The more challenging part of Christianity is to do the other things that James learned to do. James teaches that to prove that you are a true Christian, you need to repent from your sinful ways, believe in the gospel of the Kingdom of God, and follow the example of Jesus Christ as your role model.

> *James 1:19 (KJV) Wherefore, my beloved brethren, let every man be **swift to hear, slow to speak, slow to wrath**:* [Emphasis added]

> *James 1:26 (KJV) If any man among you seem to be religious, and bridleth not his tongue, but deceiveth his own heart, this man's religion is vain.*

James 3:5-6 (KJV) Even so the tongue is a little member, and boasteth great things. Behold, how great a matter a little fire kindleth! And the tongue is a fire, a world of iniquity: so is the tongue among our members, that it defileth the whole body, and setteth on fire the course of nature; and it is set on fire of hell.

James 3:8 (KJV) But the tongue can no man tame; it is an unruly evil, full of deadly poison.

James 3:2-12

For in many things we offend all. If any man offend not in word, the same is a perfect man, and able also to bridle the whole body. Behold, we put bits in the horses' mouths, that they may obey us; and we turn about their whole body. Behold also the ships, which though they be so great, and are driven of fierce winds, yet are they turned about with a very small helm, whithersoever the governor listeth. Even so the tongue is a little member, and boasteth great things. Behold, how great a matter a little fire kindleth! And the tongue is a fire, a world of iniquity: so is the tongue among our members, that it defileth the whole body, and setteth on fire the course of nature; and it is set on fire of hell. For every kind of beasts, and of birds, and of serpents, and of things in the sea, is tamed, and hath been tamed of mankind: But the tongue can no man tame; it is an unruly evil, full of deadly poison. Therewith bless we God, even the Father; and therewith curse we men, which are made after the similitude of God. Out of the same mouth proceedeth blessing and cursing. My brethren, these things ought not so to be. Doth a fountain send forth at the same place sweet water and bitter? Can the fig tree, my brethren, bear olive berries? either a vine, figs? so can no fountain both yield salt water and fresh. Who is a wise man and endued with knowledge among you? let him shew out of a good conversation his works with meekness of wisdom. But if ye have bitter envying and strife in your hearts, glory not, and lie not against the truth. This wisdom descendeth not from above, but is earthly, sensual, devilish. For where envying and strife is, there is confusion and every evil work. But the wisdom that is from above is first pure, then peaceable, gentle, and easy to be intreated, full of mercy and good fruits, without partiality, and without hypocrisy. And the fruit of righteousness is sown in peace of them that make peace.

18. Conflict

James 3:2

> *For in many things we offend all. If any man offend not in word,
> the same is a perfect man, and able also to bridle the whole
> body.*

Everyone will offend someone at some time. It is not a question of *if*; it is a question of *when*. If any man can honestly claim that he has never offended anyone, that man is perfect – and a liar. Only Jesus has the right to claim that he has never sinned. *If* you can keep control of your entire body – including your tongue, *then* you might be able to come close to perfection.

When you fall and use your words to wound another, be quick to apologize. Do not attempt to explain why you said the hurtful words; the explanation will only heap live, hot coals on top of an already incendiary situation.

After you have apologized, immediately do your best to break the bad habit of speaking evil words. Do not speak evil to anyone or about anyone.

James 3:3-4

> *Behold, we put bits in the horses' mouths, that they may obey
> us; and we turn about their whole body. Behold also the ships,
> which though they be so great, and are driven of fierce winds,
> yet are they turned about with a very small helm,
> whithersoever the governor listeth.*

James 3:5-6

> *Even so the tongue is a little member, and boasteth great
> things. Behold, how great a matter a little fire kindleth! And the
> tongue is a fire, a world of iniquity: so is the tongue among our
> members, that it defileth the whole body, and setteth on fire the
> course of nature; and it is set on fire of hell.*

Just like the small bit in the horse's mouth controls the horse's large body (James 3:3–4) and the very small rudder controls the direction of the large ship (James 3:5–6), the small tongue controls the direction of your relationships.

Just as a tiny spark can ignite a vast and uncontrollable forest fire, a small tongue can ignite a huge and uncontrollable conflict, argument, fight, or war.

James 3:7-8

For every kind of beasts, and of birds, and of serpents, and of things in the sea, is tamed, and hath been tamed of mankind: But the tongue can no man tame; it is an unruly evil, full of deadly poison.

Man can subdue or tame many animals, but the tongue cannot be subdued or tamed. In fact, the negative words expressed by the tongue are often full of evil and deadly poison (James 3:7–8).

The negative words expressed by the tongue can poison the speaker as well as the listener. When your teenage son or daughter speaks nasty things to you as a parent, it is not only the tongue but the speaker's entire body that is punished. The negative message of the son or daughter produces more damage than a similar negative message from someone outside of the family.

When a husband or wife continually speaks negative messages to their spouse, the tongue and the entire body of the speaker are divorced. The negative message of the husband or wife produces more damage than a similar negative message from someone outside of the family.

James 3:9-10

Therewith bless we God, even the Father; and therewith curse we men, which are made after the similitude of God. Out of the same mouth proceedeth blessing and cursing. My brethren, these things ought not so to be.

How can we praise God and, with the same mouth, curse men who are made in the image of God? *If* a man is made in the image of God, *then* cursing our fellow man is the same as cursing God.

18. Conflict

Remember that God loves all people made in his image, even if they deliberately or mistakenly choose to follow evil instead of righteousness.

James 3:11-12

Doth a fountain send forth at the same place sweet water and bitter? Can the fig tree, my brethren, bear olive berries? either a vine, figs? so can no fountain both yield salt water and fresh.

The tongue is uniquely capable of expressing both negative and positive, as well as both curses and praises. The words released from the tongue are expressions of the condition of the heart. *If* the heart is evil, *then* the words will be evil. *If* the heart is righteous, *then* the words will be righteous.

Just as a water spring cannot release both sweet and salty water, a righteous heart will likely not release both negative and positive messages to fellow man.

Just as a fig tree cannot bear olives, a righteous heart will likely not release both negative and positive messages to fellow man.

James 3:13-18

Who is a wise man and endued with knowledge among you? let him shew out of a good conversation his works with meekness of wisdom. But if ye have bitter envying and strife in your hearts, glory not, and lie not against the truth. This wisdom descendeth not from above, but is earthly, sensual, devilish. For where envying and strife is, there is confusion and every evil work. But the wisdom that is from above is first pure, then peaceable, gentle, and easy to be intreated, full of mercy and good fruits, without partiality, and without hypocrisy. And the fruit of righteousness is sown in peace of them that make peace.

Only with God's Wisdom and God's Righteousness can we have any hope of coming close to controlling the tongue.

We must continually guard our hearts and our tongues. Children are not born with saintly behaviour and must be taught Kingdom Principles. Many stimuli can cause even the most righteous of hearts to falter and become evil. As the heart becomes evil, the tongue speaks evil.

The speaker's hurtful words will poison the speaker's mind as well as the mind of the listener. As the speaker repeatedly speaks poisonous words, their heart internalizes this poison, and their heart becomes filled with more evil, starting a downward spiral to self-destruction.

Do not speak evil to anyone or about anyone. Even if the person being spoken about does not hear the words, the speaker's mind and heart will hear and feel the words and poison the speaker's heart to become evil. *If* we extend the teachings of Jesus Christ to know that thinking of sin is also sin, *then* we must also stop thinking evil words about anyone. Your thoughts lead to your words, which, in turn, lead to your actions. Your actions impact your relationships and society. You can change your relationship and society simply by changing your thoughts.

Dreams come from our unconscious thoughts. If, in a dream, I feel angry towards someone who has harmed me in real life, I pray to God for forgiveness. It is not okay to express angry emotions towards someone. It is not okay to think angry thoughts towards someone. Therefore, it is not okay to dream of angry emotions toward someone.

INTROVERTED
PEOPLE
TASK
EXTROVERTED

19. Resolving Conflicts

Opposites often do attract: introverted with extroverted; task-oriented with people-oriented. Even though there is a romantic line that says, "You complete me," couples should never look to complete each other because the jagged edges of one individual's personality style can never perfectly match the jagged edges of another individual's personality style. God is the only one with a love strong enough to be a perfect match to the jagged edges of each individual.

I have heard it said that a marriage is not truly a marriage until conflict enters the marriage. No two people can live together without disagreements, but conflict does not need to end a marriage if the two spouses are willing to become more Christ-like.

Disagreements are guaranteed to occur; however, conflicts are a choice. With good interpersonal skills, it is possible to prevent escalation from disagreement to conflict. It takes two people to have a conflict, and it takes two people to resolve the conflict. And it will take two people to grow together to avoid future conflicts.

Marriage is a divine blessing. Faith and marriage are made of the same key ingredients. Faith = Love + Belief + Trust + Hope. God does not cause tribulations, but God uses tribulations to grow your spirit and faith. And you need faith to help you overcome the tribulation.

It is easy to comprehend that you need to believe, trust, and hope in God to expand the circle of your comfort zone. You also need faith to receive the blessings that God would like to bestow upon you and upon your marriage. Pretending or Faking-fine is a rejection of God's Blessings and a refusal to allow God to work miracles in you and, by extension, in your marriage.

19. Resolving Conflicts

Just as you need love, belief, trust, and hope to establish a strong faith, you need love, belief, trust, and hope to establish a strong marriage.

Never threaten or attempt to control another individual. I know from personal experience that I do not like to be threatened, manipulated, or controlled.

When I was seventeen years old, my girlfriend and I had an argument. She had lied to me, and I was taking time to consider if the lie was serious enough to end the relationship.

The day after the argument, my girlfriend came to my house pretending to visit with my sister. I was in the basement talking with my best friend. My girlfriend walked into the room, walked up to my best friend, gave him a hello kiss on the cheek, and then walked out of the room without saying a word to me.

My friend looked at me and said, "I didn't do anything."

I said, "I think she was trying to make me jealous, so if you would like to take her out, she is all yours."

My girlfriend was quite upset when she learned that her manipulative strategy had backfired. I am sure that other people have had experiences.

It is important to do everything possible to resolve disagreements before they escalate into conflicts. However, even conflicts and wars can be resolved. Resolving conflict is always easier when the issues are still small disagreements and before any criticism or defensiveness has been triggered.

This section's strategies for resolving conflict work best when the people are committed and mature enough to use the tools. Spouses need to unite spiritually in their Spiritual Minds, Hearts, and Wills as well as physically in their bodies.

Romans 12:2 (KJV) And be not conformed to this world: but be ye transformed by the renewing of your mind, that ye may prove what is that good, and acceptable, and perfect, will of God.

Philippians 2:2-5 (KJV) Fulfil ye my joy, that ye be likeminded, having the same love, being of one accord, of one mind. Let nothing be done through strife or vainglory; but in lowliness of mind let each esteem other better than themselves. Look not every man on his own things, but every man also on the things of others. Let this mind be in you, which was also in Christ Jesus:

Control your mind's thoughts to change your Spiritual Heart's feelings, which will, in turn, change your Spiritual Will. Thoughts become beliefs that produce more thoughts supporting and reinforcing the belief. The patterns of your thoughts, in support of a belief, are like obsessive-compulsive disorder (OCD) for the mind. Your words reflect the thoughts of your Spiritual Mind. Your emotions reflect the feelings of your Spiritual Heart. Your actions and non-actions reflect your Spiritual Will. In turn, your Spiritual Will reflects your Spiritual Mind and your Spiritual Heart in a circular relationship.

The Spiritual Mind feeds the Spiritual Heart; the Spiritual Heart feeds the Spiritual Will. Spoken words reflect thoughts that come from the Spiritual Mind. Emoted emotions reflect feelings that come from the Spiritual Heart. Observable actions of the Spiritual Will reflect the desires of the Spiritual Heart and beliefs of the Spiritual Mind.

If sixty to ninety percent of your adversary's words are negative, or *if* sixty to ninety percent of your adversary's emotions are negative, or *if* sixty to ninety percent of your adversary's actions and non-actions are negative, *then* you know that your adversary is a RATS or Crazy-Maker.

If sixty to ninety percent of your thoughts and words are negative, or *if* sixty to ninety percent of your feelings and emotions are negative, or *if* sixty to ninety percent of your actions and non-actions are negative, *then* you know that you are a RATS or Crazy-Maker.

You should be able to receive eighty to ninety percent positive words, emotions, actions and non-actions from your STAR. As a STAR, you should be able to give eighty to ninety percent positive words, emotions, actions and non-actions.

> *Proverbs 16:3 (KJV) Commit thy works unto the LORD, and thy thoughts shall be established.*

The good news is that Proverbs 16:3 teaches that you don't need to feel eighty to ninety percent positive to fix things. Fake it till you make it. Just follow the rules in the Holy Bible, and you will become a STAR, reducing conflicts and thereby improving relationships.

The Spiritual Will feeds the Spiritual Heart; the Spiritual Heart feeds the Spiritual Mind. Observable actions and non-actions change the desires of the Spiritual Heart and beliefs of the Spiritual Mind. Emoted emotions change the feelings of the Spiritual Heart. Spoken words change the thoughts of the Spiritual Mind. *If* you know that you need to learn empathy towards others in order to become a STAR, *then* behave as if you feel empathy and observe their reactions to your words and behaviour until the neurons of your brain are rewired, and your empathy becomes real.

Whatever starting point in the circular relationship of your Spiritual Mind, Heart and Will, righteous input is always the correct input to achieve righteous output. The Holy Bible is the only correct definition of righteous behaviour.

Add God and Stir

> *John 13:34 (KJV) A new commandment I give unto you, That ye love one another; as I have loved you, that ye also love one another.*

The Holy Bible teaches that Jesus gives us a new commandment: love one another as he loved us.

It is important to remember the distinction between feelings and emotions. The emotion of love is not the same as the feeling of love. Emotions require decision, commitment and spiritual obedience. The only way that families can have true harmony is by becoming one with Jesus Christ and following Jesus' light to the spiritual Kingdom of Heaven on Earth.

Matthew 12:46-50 (KJV) While he yet talked to the people, behold, his mother and his brethren stood without, desiring to speak with him. Then one said unto him, Behold, thy mother and thy brethren stand without, desiring to speak with thee. But he answered and said unto him that told him, Who is my mother? and who are my brethren? And he stretched forth his hand toward his disciples, and said, Behold my mother and my brethren! For whosoever shall do the will of my Father which is in heaven, the same is my brother, and sister, and mother.

Matthew 10:5, 34-38 (KJV) These twelve Jesus sent forth, and commanded them, saying, Go not into the way of the Gentiles, and into any city of the Samaritans enter ye not: Think not that I am come to send peace on earth: I came not to send peace, but a sword. For I am come to set a man at variance against his father, and the daughter against her mother, and the daughter in law against her mother in law. And a man's foes shall be they of his own household. He that loveth father or mother more than me is not worthy of me: and he that loveth son or daughter more than me is not worthy of me. And he that taketh not his cross, and followeth after me, is not worthy of me.

The Holy Bible teaches that we should choose God's righteousness over our loved ones' evil. *If* families do not unite with Jesus Christ, *then* our Kingdom Assignment is more important than remaining in harmful, damaging families.

If your family follows the way of the RATSs or Crazy-Makers, *then* you must strike out on a solo journey to achieve your individual Kingdom Assignment. Each family member has an individual Kingdom Assignment, and they jointly have a family Kingdom Assignment. God had a plan for bringing you together with your *family of origin* and your *family of marriage*.

There really is no need to have conflict within your family if you follow Jesus' example. It is important to remember that walking away is <u>not</u> always a permanent physical walking away but might be a temporary spiritual walking away. It is also important to remember that everyone makes mistakes and that forgiveness is mandatory. So, it may often be better to walk away temporarily as a form of spiritual timeout.

Proverbs 12:18 (KJV) There is that speaketh like the piercings of a sword: but the tongue of the wise is health.

Proverbs 18:21 (KJV) Death and life are in the power of the tongue: and they that love it shall eat the fruit thereof.

The Holy Bible teaches us to guard the weapon that we call our tongues. Listening to the words of a poisonous tongue is unhealthy for our bodies. There are many examples in the Holy Bible of Jesus healing people's spirits in order to heal their bodies.

A friend told me a fictional story that explains the damage of conflict. There was a teenage boy who dealt with conflict by raging on the people around him. An elderly neighbour suggested to the boy that, instead of raging, he should hammer a nail into the elderly neighbour's fence. The boy accepted the elderly man's offer, and because the boy took out his rage on the nail, his relationships with people around him improved.

One day, the boy came back to the elderly neighbour, explaining that he no longer felt the need to rage. The elderly neighbour suggested that whenever the boy successfully conquered his urge to rage, he should come and remove a nail from the fence.

After some time, the boy noticed that the removal of many nails left behind many holes. When he commented on this, the elderly neighbour explained that rage causes damage that needs to be repaired.

It is easier to avoid the damage of rage <u>before</u> the damage occurs than to repair the damage <u>after</u> the lesson of anger management has been learned.

Isaiah 26:3 (KJV) Thou wilt keep him in perfect peace, whose mind is stayed on thee: because he trusteth in thee.

Colossians 3:2 (KJV) Set your affection on things above, not on things on the earth.

*Philippians 4:8 (KJV) Finally, brethren, **whatsoever things are true, whatsoever things are honest, whatsoever things are just, whatsoever things are pure, whatsoever things are lovely, whatsoever things are of good report; if there be any virtue, and if there be any praise, think on these things**. [Emphasis added]*

In reality, you are not contending against the carnal, living opponent in your conflict; you are actually contending against Satan and the negative feelings that arise in you. Jesus did not promise a peaceful life – only a peaceful way to examine the issue with God's Help.

The Christian life can be like standing in the eye of a hurricane. The conflict is the storm raging around you while you are focused on God's Beauty and Peace. You see the storm from the peaceful, godly center of your Spiritual Mind, Heart, and Will.

The eye of the hurricane is filled with a special calm companionship in the presence of God, the Holy Spirit, and Jesus Christ. In the presence of the Godhead is God's Divine Wisdom, Understanding, Knowledge, Strength, Courage, Love, Faith, Joy, Peace, Empathy, and Harmony.

Never speak in the heat of the moment when your feelings are negative and intense. If you cannot speak calmly in a soft-spoken, gentle, loving tone, you must walk away from the incident until you can speak calmly.

Discussing your relationship challenges with a professional psychotherapist is always a good idea. I have heard several psychotherapists say that they seek other psychotherapists when they need help. Somehow, being in the trenches of conflict requires the assistance of an objective expert to help resolve some conflicts.

Never discuss your private relationship issues with your friends or relatives unless they are a psychotherapist.

Discussing your relationship issues with friends and relatives is a strategy of might over right. Your friends and relatives will always be biased toward your feelings, and they might not know how to dig deep enough into the details to find the real issue. They might also keep you trapped in the rut of that issue; every time you visit them, they might bring the focus back to the negative feelings of that issue.

Another reason not to discuss your relationship incidents with friends and relatives is that it will probably increase tension between you and your spouse. You will have expanded the scope of the conflict to you and your friends against your spouse, and the conflict will take on a life of its own. You strengthen Satan's arm against your spouse, making your spouse more desperate and making reconciliation more difficult.

Another reason against discussing your relationship issues with friends and relatives is that you will effectively transfer devils, demons, and other evil entities from your spirit to your friends and relatives. This behaviour might establish or escalate the conflict in your friends' and relatives' relationships.

When you marry in a Christian church, you and your spouse are no longer considered two separate spirits. You are now one spirit in two bodies. You are one spirit in two bodies against a world that is motivated by greed and power to prevent your spiritual growth. Your friends and relatives might be nominal Christians who are in the world and of the world; nominal Christians are not suitable for your spiritual growth even though they call themselves Christians.

"Couples who know how to play and have fun together develop a bond that can carry them through the most difficult of times." Dr. Steve Stephens.

Romans 12:2 (KJV) And be not conformed to this world: but be ye transformed by the renewing of your mind, that ye may prove what is that good, and acceptable, and perfect, will [desire] of God. [Clarification terms added]

Being popular with people in the world will never be your Kingdom Assignment.

There is an expression that says, "You can predict your future by looking at your friends." At the time of writing this book, divorce rates in Canada were thirty-eight percent. If your friends are divorced or in codependent marriages, looking to them for advice will likely result in you also becoming divorced or codependent in your marriage.

Be very careful about who you allow into your inner circle. Society, government, and businesses use direct and indirect influence to restrict spiritual growth. RATSs and Crazy-Makers are actually easier to control than mature STARs because the troubling behaviour of RATSs and Crazy-Makers justifies tighter controls and more militant tactics. RATSs and Crazy-Makers produce more RATSs and Crazy-Makers. RATSs and Crazy-Makers are always willing to occupy positions of authority where their harmful skill set will be allowed, appreciated, and rewarded.

Proverbs 25:21-22 (KJV) If thine enemy be hungry, give him bread to eat; and if he be thirsty, give him water to drink: For thou shalt heap coals of fire upon his head, and the LORD shall reward thee.

Romans 12:20 (KJV) Therefore if thine enemy hunger, feed him; if he thirst, give him drink: for in so doing thou shalt heap coals of fire on his head.

Matthew 7:13-14 (KJV) Enter ye in at the strait gate: for wide is the gate, and broad is the way, that leadeth to destruction, and many there be which go in thereat: Because strait is the gate, and narrow is the way, which leadeth unto life, and few there be that find it.

Matthew 7:21-23 (KJV) Not every one that saith unto me, Lord, Lord, shall enter into the kingdom of heaven; but he that doeth the will of my Father which is in heaven. Many will say to me in that day, Lord, Lord, have we not prophesied in thy name? and in thy name have cast out devils? and in thy name done many wonderful works? And then will I profess unto them, I never knew you: depart from me, ye that work iniquity.

Matthew 7:24-29 (KJV) Therefore whosoever heareth these sayings of mine, and doeth them, I will liken him unto a wise man, which built his house upon a rock: And the rain descended, and the floods came, and the winds blew, and beat upon that house; and it fell not: for it was founded upon a rock. And every one that heareth these sayings of mine, and doeth them not, shall be likened unto a foolish man, which built his house upon the sand: And the rain descended, and the floods came, and the winds blew, and beat upon that house; and it fell: and great was the fall of it. And it came to pass, when Jesus had ended these sayings, the people were astonished at his doctrine: For he taught them as one having authority, and not as the scribes.

Matthew 7:13-14 and 7:21-29 teach us always to do the right thing, even when it is difficult or unpopular.

*Deuteronomy 6:17-19 (KJV) Ye shall diligently keep the commandments of the LORD your God, and his testimonies, and his statutes, which he hath commanded thee. **And thou shalt do that which is right and good in the sight of the LORD: that it may be well with thee**, and that thou mayest go in and possess the good land which the LORD sware unto thy fathers, To cast out all thine enemies from before thee, as the LORD hath spoken. [Emphasis added]*

If you are having difficulty with anyone, especially a RATS or a Crazy-Maker or enemy, always do the right thing based on Kingdom Principles.

A woman talked to me about her difficult situation. While she was about to get into her car to escape her abusive husband, he grabbed her head and smashed her head through the driver's side window. In her situation, asking this woman to stay with her husband and pray would be irresponsible.

If there is a possible danger to your spirit or body, *then* walk away, or let the RATS or Crazy-Maker walk away from you. Deal with the conflict resolution from a safe distance.

When a man is abusive to his wife, the Holy Bible describes him as a wicked man and does not give him the title of husband. The title of husband is reserved for a man behaving righteously.

If this situation cannot be resolved by spiritually walking away, and *if* reconciliation is the goal, *then* physically walking away as a temporary timeout is the right thing to do. Eventually, always doing the right thing will frustrate the RATS or Crazy-Maker into giving up their tactics. In any case, if you have obeyed the Kingdom Principles, you have not compromised the integrity of your spirit.

Luke 22:39-46 (KJV) And he came out, and went, as he was wont, to the mount of Olives; and his disciples also followed him. And when he was at the place, he said unto them, Pray that ye enter not into temptation. And he was withdrawn from them about a stone's cast, and kneeled down, and prayed, Saying, **Father, if thou be willing, remove this cup from me: nevertheless not my will, but thine, be done.** *And there appeared an angel unto him from heaven, strengthening him.* **And being in an agony he prayed more earnestly: and his sweat was as it were great drops of blood falling down to the ground.** *And when he rose up from prayer, and was come to his disciples, he found them sleeping for sorrow, And said unto them, Why sleep ye? rise and pray, lest ye enter into temptation. [Emphasis added]*

Luke 22:39-46 is an excellent example of the struggle between feelings and emotions. The Holy Bible describes Jesus' physical condition the night that he was arrested; he was experiencing the agonizing tribulation of his pending death, and "his sweat was as it were great drops of blood falling down to the ground."

It is important to remember that the circumstances of Luke 22:39-46 occurred in early spring when the air temperature was still cool. Also, it was nighttime and at the foot of a mountain. Jesus' sweat was not due to the air temperature.

What Jesus was feeling is intuitively obvious. Jesus knew that he would be killed, and his body reacted with a strong feeling of desire to escape death.

However, Jesus said, "Father, if thou be willing, remove this cup from me: nevertheless not my will, but thine, be done." In response to Jesus' prayer, God sent an angel to strengthen Jesus; "And there appeared an angel unto him from heaven, strengthening him."

Jesus had a Kingdom Assignment, and no matter how much the feelings of his natural body desired to use self-will to escape his Kingdom Assignment, Jesus' Spiritual Mind, Heart, and Will were united and resolved to express the emotion of determination to do the right thing.

Jesus needed to call on his Action Personality Style to remain resolved and do God's Will. The carnal *feeling* of love for God's People was not enough to enable Jesus to complete his Kingdom Assignment. It was the spiritual *emotion* of love, which requires a decision, that enabled Jesus to remain committed to his Kingdom Assignment.

We need to learn to never react to our feelings. Just as Jesus did, we each have a duty to process our feelings through our Spiritual Mind, Heart, and Will, to make a decision, commit to doing the right thing, and respond with the correct emotion to the unpleasant circumstance.

Before approaching a trespasser to discuss a trespass, pray to God for guidance. When you start the <u>conversation</u> with the trespasser, you should allow them an opportunity to pray to God for guidance. Then, before addressing the root of the trespass, you should both pray <u>together</u> to bring God into the conversation.

Luke 6:35-38 (KJV) ... love ye your enemies, and do good, and lend, hoping for nothing again; and your reward shall be great, and ye shall be the children of the Highest: for he is kind unto the unthankful and to the evil. Be ye therefore merciful, as your Father also is merciful. Judge not, and ye shall not be judged: condemn not, and ye shall not be condemned: forgive, and ye

*shall be forgiven: Give, and it shall be given unto you; good
measure, pressed down, and shaken together, and running
over, shall men give into your bosom. For with the same
measure that ye mete withal it shall be measured to you again.*

Luke 6:35-38 teaches us to love, do good and be gener-
ous with our abundance, as God is loving, kind, and merciful to
us. The reward for your righteousness will come from God.

Start preparing now for the pending disagreement or
conflict that is guaranteed to come up. It costs nothing to give
praise and compliments, and it only takes seconds to speak
words of praise and compliments that can last a lifetime. However, resolving hurtful words takes hours, days, or years.

Every marriage has a joint account in the 'Love Fidelity
and Trust.' Into your joint account at the 'Love Fidelity and
Trust,' you need to continuously deposit words of praise, compliments, honour, and deposits of soft-spoken words, righteous
words, encouraging words, and cheerleading words.

Words of complaint, gaslighting, yelling, backstabbing,
badmouthing, and name-calling are withdrawals from your joint
account at the 'Love Fidelity and Trust.'

If you allow the joint account to fall into overdraft with
more withdrawals than deposits, the bank account might be
closed and the marriage dissolved.

It is not only words that affect the balance in the joint
account at the 'Love Fidelity and Trust.' Remember that we
tend to judge our own behaviour based on our intent. Remember
also that we tend to determine another's intentions based only
on our perception of their observable behaviour and then judge
based on our perception of their intentions.

If we allow negative thoughts about our spouse to linger
in our minds, *then* our thoughts will colour our perception of
their intent. Then, we attack them with evidence of something
based only on our perceptions.

Proverbs 23:7 says, "For as he thinketh in his heart, so
is he ...." The thoughts of your Spiritual Mind feed your Spir-

itual Heart, which feeds your Spiritual Will. *If* the Spiritual Mind feeds negative thoughts about your spouse to your Spiritual Heart, *then* your heart will become negative toward your spouse.

If your Spiritual Mind feeds positive thoughts about your spouse to your Spiritual Heart, *then* your heart will become positive toward your spouse. When your heart is positive toward your spouse, it will be easier to pause and consider the possibility that you have misinterpreted their intentions when they do something hurtful to you.

In Luke 6:35-38, Jesus warns that we will be judged as we judge others. Instead of judging, we are instructed to forgive. Holy Scripture also teaches us to resolve issues before going to a judge. Instead, work together to grow and become Kingdom of Heaven STARs. Reconciliation of trespasses between two STARs should be possible without God's Intervention.

I believe that the term judge in the New Testament refers to a judge outside the Jewish community, so judgments would not be based on God's Laws.

*Genesis 2:5 (KJV) And every plant of the field before it was in the earth, and every herb of the field before it grew: for the LORD God had not caused it to rain upon the earth, and **there was not a man to till the ground**. [Emphasis added].*

*Genesis 2:7 (KJV) And **the LORD God formed man of the dust of the ground**, and breathed into his nostrils the breath of life; and man became a living soul. [Emphasis added]*

Genesis 2:18 (KJV) And the LORD God said, It is not good that the man should be alone; I will make him an help meet [suitable] for him. [Clarification terms added]

*Genesis 2:21-24 (KJV) And the LORD God caused a deep sleep to fall upon Adam, and he slept: and he took one of his ribs, and closed up the flesh instead thereof; **And the rib, which the LORD God had taken from man, made he a woman, and brought her unto the man**. And Adam said, This is now bone of my bones, and flesh of my flesh: she shall be called Woman, because she was taken out of Man. Therefore shall a man leave his father and his mother, and*

shall cleave unto his wife: and they shall be one flesh.
[Emphasis added]

Adam was charged with the duty of being a steward of God's Earth. Eve was charged with the duty of helping Adam. So, both Adam and Eve had been charged with the duty of being stewards of God's Earth.

A marriage is like a garden. The husband and the wife have been charged with the duty of caring for the garden of their marriage. Both should prepare against possible damaging conflict by showering each other with at least one compliment or praise every day.

Remember that it takes at least ten compliments to recover from every small criticism. *If* the criticism is very hurtful, *then* it might take a thousand compliments to heal your marriage. Remember every criticism, complaint, name-calling, and backstabbing that you threw at your spouse. Any negative emotion thrown at your spouse is like a weed, and some weeds are more invasive than others.

If you are a gardener and *if* you have experienced binder weed, *then* you know how difficult it is to remove it. Treat every negative emotion as if it were a binder weed root that you are about to plant into the garden of your marriage.

*Proverbs 4:20-27 (KJV) My son, attend to my words; incline thine ear unto my sayings. Let them not depart from thine eyes; keep them in the midst of thine heart. For they are life unto those that find them, and health to all their flesh. **Keep thy heart with all diligence; for out of it are the issues of life**. Put away from thee a froward mouth, and perverse lips put far from thee. Let thine eyes look right on, and let thine eyelids look straight before thee. Ponder the path of thy feet, and let all thy ways be established. Turn not to the right hand nor to the left: remove thy foot from evil. [Emphasis added]*

Remember also that a compliment should match the spouse's primary personality style. Though saying please and thank you is always important, it is important to remember that saying "Thank you" is only an expression of appreciation. It is not a compliment, nor is it praise. You say "Thank you" to the server at the restaurant, but it is highly unlikely that you will climb into bed with the restaurant server!

Remember that your spouse might already be thinking negative thoughts about themselves, and your negative emotion might be enough to put the nail in the coffin of their self-image. It is very easy to comprehend that your words are generated from the thoughts that you have been feeding into your heart. However, it is important to know that the words that you speak to your spouse become thoughts in their Spiritual Mind, which in turn feed their Spiritual Heart. Hearing hurtful words becomes the thoughts that feed poison into their hearts. Wounded hearts require lots of loving care and lots of time to recover.

Remember also that God loves the individual with whom you have a conflict. *If* the other individual is honestly attempting to resolve the conflict, *then* they can be your ally against the same carnal evil.

Join forces to fight the real evil. Bring in God's Army of angels as your reinforcements to fight Satan's evil.

With God, all things are possible. But Jesus beheld them, and said unto them, "With men this is impossible; but with God all things are possible." (Matthew 19:28) Jesus said unto him, "If thou canst believe, all things are possible to him that believeth." (Mark 9:23) And Jesus looking upon them saith, "With men it is impossible, but not with God: for with God all things are possible." (Mark 10:27)

> *Romans 12:17-18 (KJV) Recompense to no man evil for evil. Provide things honest in the sight of all men. If it be possible, as much as lieth in you, live peaceably with all men.*

Romans 12:18 instructs us to live peaceably with all men, and women, of course; this is especially true in marriage. A marriage is not real until the tribulation of conflict enters into the union to grow and strengthen the marriage.

You cannot truly appreciate the good times unless you accept and deal with the challenging times. Conflict resolution is the price that must be paid for deeper intimacy. At any stage of marriage, take all steps necessary, including learning new skills, to protect the future of your marriage.

1 Corinthians 14:9 (KJV) So likewise ye, except ye utter by the tongue words easy to be understood, how shall it be known what is spoken? for ye shall speak into the air.

Seven percent of conflict is due to words, and ninety-three percent is due to the delivery (quality of voice and body language) of the message.

MT 6:33 But seek ye first the kingdom of God, and his righteousness; and all these things shall be added unto you.

What would Jesus do? Jesus is a Kingdom of Heaven STAR and can use the correct personality style for every situation.

It is not about finding the spouse that best matches your personality style; it is finding the spouse who can grow to become a Kingdom of Heaven STAR with you. It is not about giving your spouse what they need based on their personality style; it is about both spouses being able to use whatever personality style best fits the circumstances.

Instead of fighting our differences, we should accept each other as teachers and model the positive differences between us so that we can both have the opportunity to become Kingdom of Heaven STARs.

Positive learning is the incorporation of positive differences into our character. Negative learning is avoiding negative differences to ensure that the other individual's negative differences never come into our character.

My dad's Action Personality Style has positive aspects that I would like to incorporate into my character. My dad always seemed fearless, very determined, and goal-oriented. My Action Personality Style is still developing.

My dad's Action Personality Style also has negative aspects that I have long ago removed from my character.

Solutions for relationship disagreements and conflicts are not possible without Empathy. Empathy can be learned by following the rules found in the Holy Bible.

I can tell you from personal experience that adhering to the rules is difficult in the heat of conflict, so the <u>first</u> rule that you need to remember is to walk away for a timeout if you feel angry, hurt or have any other negative emotion.

Before you address the conflict, you must decide to fight fair. Never fight in the heat of the moment; you will say things that you will regret. Always give your partner time to calm down before asking for a discussion.

After you and your partner are calm, review the rules found in this book, review the DESK procedure, and pray to God for guidance to help find a resolution. Then, ask your spouse for a DESK session.

20. How to Fight Fair

I hope that it is self-evident that fighting fair is a term for verbal arguments and not physical fights; I hope there are no physical fights in your relationships. *If* your conflict has escalated to physical fights, *then* remove yourself to a safe distance and invoke a timeout for everyone to calm down. Once everyone is calm, you are now ready to start discussions to resolve the conflict.

Always do the right thing. This decision means always doing things according to the Kingdom Principles, as revealed in the Holy Bible. Always use your will to fight with integrity, with your Spiritual Mind and Heart united by God's Mind and Heart, to achieve the best results.

Every room in your home should be a safe zone. This rule is especially true for the bedrooms and the dining room. I have taught the DESK method to several families. One Christian family uses their garage for their standing DESK conflict resolution meetings. If you were called to the garage, you knew that it was probably for a DESK conflict resolution meeting. Using the garage for DESK meetings had the advantage of keeping the meetings short because the meetings were standing meetings.

Satan is a great deceiver and will do anything that he can to get you focused on everyone else as the cause of the conflict. Satan always promises big but delivers small.

God gave everyone free will, and we can only truly control ourselves. God gifted you with free will, and nobody has the right to override your free will. This right to free will does not mean that you have the right to choose sin. Sin usually violates someone else's free will or causes pain. You do not have the right to use your free will to violate someone else's free will or well-being.

Unfortunately, you might choose to use your free will to relinquish your free will. You might allow another to use their free will to override your free will. You might choose to remain in a relationship that violates your boundaries and causes you pain.

Exodus 20:3-5 (KJV) **Thou shalt have no other gods before me**. *Thou shalt not make unto thee any graven image, or any likeness of any thing that is in heaven above, or that is in the earth beneath, or that is in the water under the earth:* **Thou shalt not bow down thyself to them, nor serve them**: *for I the LORD thy God am a jealous God, visiting the iniquity of the fathers upon the children unto the third and fourth generation of them that hate me; [Emphasis Added]*

Submitting yourself to someone else's free will is a violation of God's First and Second Commandments: "Thou shalt have no other God before me" and "Thou shalt not make unto thee any graven image … nor bow down to the images nor serve them". By submitting your will to another's will, you are accepting this other individual as your God.

King Solomon wrote in the book of Ecclesiastes chapter 4:

Again, I considered all travail, and every right work, that for this a man is envied of his neighbour. This is also vanity and vexation of spirit. The fool foldeth his hands together, and eateth his own flesh. Better is an handful with quietness, than both the hands full with travail and vexation of spirit. Two are better than one; because they have a good reward for their labour. For if they fall, the one will lift up his fellow: but woe to him that is alone when he falleth; for he hath not another to help him up. Again, if two lie together, then they have heat: but how can one be warm alone? And if one prevail against him, two shall withstand him; and a threefold cord is not quickly broken.

King Solomon suggests that struggling against each other to achieve an enviably perfect goal can only achieve vanity (wasted effort) and vexation of spirit (unresolvable spiritual irritation).

When we focus on our adversary as the cause of a conflict, the only possible solution is to force a change in *their* behaviour, which is a wasted effort (vanity) that can never be successful (vexation of spirit). The conflict can never be resolved, and therefore, it is spiritual irritation (vexation of spirit) that can only grow with each incident.

It may be possible to force a concession on the others involved in the conflict, but the final result will be a bigger conflict in the future.

Divorce or the end of a relationship is not always the correct answer. King Solomon suggests that giving up and doing nothing, like a fool who folds his arms across his chest in a closed stance, will be self-destructive.

King Solomon suggests that the best solution is to be satisfied with one handful of agreement rather than two handfuls of forced concessions with endless strife (travail) and an irritated spirit (vexation of spirit).

King Solomon also suggests that two people working together in cooperation against the true issue of the conflict can result in true satisfaction for both. In cooperation, they must recognize the strengths of the other and agree on a solution that uses their respective strengths. In cooperation, they must unite against Satan as the true enemy and producer of the conflict.

Including God in the conflict as the third strand in a threefold cord guarantees a stronger and more satisfying solution.

> *Proverbs 17:14 (KJV) The beginning of strife is as when one letteth out water: therefore leave off contention, before it be meddled with.*

King Solomon also suggests that to avoid conflict, you should walk away until you can focus on the conflict without strife and without contention. *If* you can focus on the conflict as the problem, with your spouse as your ally, and speak about the issue without any negative emotion toward your spouse, *then you can start resolving* the issue.

The solution is simple. *If* you imagine that your team is comprised of you, the other Individual, and God, and *if* you imagine the trespass and Satan as the Opponent Team, *then* you are almost always guaranteed to overcome the trespass. Then, you can continue your journey to the next challenge, where you can repeat the same successful strategy. Implementing the solution is not easy.

I recommend the DESK system for Difficult Conversations and Conflict Resolution as a strategy to fight fair.

DESK - Setting the Foundation

Before I start describing the DESK strategy for fighting fair, I think it is important to review DESK preparation.

Ephesians 5:20-21 (KJV) Giving thanks always for all things unto God and the Father in the name of our Lord Jesus Christ; **Submitting yourselves one to another in the fear of God.** *[Emphasis added]*

The foundational principle of the DESK system for Difficult Conversations and Conflict Resolution is found in Ephesians 5:20-21. The DESK system cannot succeed without mutual submission, or better translated as mutual respect, in the fear of God.

As part of submitting yourselves to each other and God, I think it is important to declare that you love God. I remember that the first time that I declared, "God, I love you," I had an uncomfortable feeling that my declaration was inappropriate. English only has one word for love, whereas Greek has many words for love. However, the three most common biblical words for love are derived from these Greek words: Eros is romantic love, Agape is godly love, and Philos is platonic love.

Eros is a *feeling* experienced by the body and, therefore, temporary. Agape is an *emotion* of unconditional love experienced after making a decision; this love is as permanent as the decision to love unconditionally. Agape love is the love we feel for our father, mother, and God.

After you have declared your love for God, you need to declare your love (romantic, godly, or platonic) for your partner in the conflict. Even if you have lost your romantic (Eros) love for your partner, it is still possible to experience godly (Agape) love for your partner.

In the appendix, I have included a prayer that I often use to invite God's Love, Joy, Peace and Harmony into the DESK meeting. It is also one of the prayers that I pray each morning to invite God to guide me through the experiences of my day.

Agape love is unconditional love, and nobody can give or receive God's Unconditional Agape Love unless they first love God. With God in your marriage relationship, your marriage overflows with God's Unconditional Agape Love into your relationships with children and others around you.

DESK Goal, Preparation and Execution

The DESK solution assumes that you would like reconciliation, and not termination, of your relationship.

Forgiveness

Forgiveness is for the sufferer's benefit; the trespasser is often unaware of or possibly does not acknowledge, the pain caused by the trespass. If working with the trespasser is not possible:

1. Write a DESK-letter, then
2. Pray to God to crack open the trespasser's mind and heart and bless the unrepentant trespasser with knowledge of God's Love, Truth and Justice,
3. Pray to God to be released from the pain of the trespass, and

4. Take comfort in the knowledge that you have unleashed God's Love, Truth and Justice into the trespasser's life so that God will deal with the trespasser as God decides, and

5. Pray to God to fill the trespasser's heart to overflowing with God's Love, to allow repentance, and

6. Pray to God to fill your heart to overflowing with God's Love, to allow forgiveness, and

7. Offer the letter as a burnt offering to God.

There will be a temptation to return the same energy, whether retaliation, eye-for-eye, or revenge, to the trespasser as what you perceive was used against you. Instead, use something more powerful: God's Power. Love, repentance, and forgiveness are required for reconciliation and are more powerful to accomplish reconciliation.

Preparation (Done Individually):

1. After clearly identifying the issue, pray to God for guidance in helping you better comprehend the conflict.

2. Pray to God for help in guiding your adversary's thoughts toward reconciliation.

3. Imagine everyone involved in the conflict as members of the same team and focused on the same goal.

4. Review all of the strengths of everyone involved in the conflict. *Ignore* *all* weaknesses because this will only lead to blaming and escalating the conflict.

5. Review the desires (sources of joy) for everyone involved in the conflict.

6. Brainstorm all the *possible good reasons* that you might have missed to explain everyone else's perspective of the conflict. This habit will get you out of your focus on your own negative feelings, such as anger.

7. Brainstorm possible solutions using everyone's strengths and desires listed above in step 4.

Discussion (Done Together):

1. Ensure that your account at your 'Love Fidelity Trust' has a large enough balance to accommodate withdrawals. Remember always to spend time doing the fun

things that the other people like so that there is a reason to stay together during a conflict situation.

2. Pray to God for guidance in helping everyone achieve better cooperation and resolve the conflict.
3. Commit to always guarding your Spiritual Mind, Heart, and Will and always doing the godly thing in all of your thoughts, words, feelings, emotions, actions and non-actions.
4. Commit to always doing the godly thing without any expectation of receiving a reward from the other individual.
5. Before discussing the conflict, review good communication and conflict resolution skills to protect your future relationship.
6. Sit <u>beside</u> each other, with your arm and thigh touching the arm and thigh of your spouse. Imagine yourselves harmoniously united on the same team focused on resolving the problem.
7. To prevent escalations of anger, remember to have a timeout if tempers flare.

Seek first to comprehend, then to be understood. You have two eyes, two ears, and one mouth, so observe and listen without speaking. (*James 1* [19]*Wherefore, my beloved brethren, let every man be swift to hear, slow to speak, slow to wrath*). Ask questions to learn what is really happening.

Listen without defending. Speak without offending.

D.E.S.K.

Over the years, I have worked as a patient with several counsellors. Some have different conflict resolution systems. Two of the systems of conflict resolution that I have been exposed to are the DESK approach and the WIN approach. I like the acronym "WIN," which stands for:

- *W*hen you…;
- *I* feel…;
- I *N*eed…

But I know the DESK approach best. The conflict resolution acronym is not important. However, *if* your counsellor is not teaching conflict resolution, *then* you might be better served by another counsellor who teaches conflict Resolution.

In every conflict, everyone is at fault to varying degrees. Therefore, everyone needs to grow in their STAR Personality Styles. *If* the counsellor is unwilling or unable to identify areas where you both need improvement, *then* you might be better served by another counsellor.

The DESK acronym stands for:

- *D*escribe the <u>observable facts</u> only
- *E*xpress your feelings with "<u>I feel</u> ..." statements
- Be *S*pecific to the <u>one issue</u> identified
- *K*eep at it until you <u>achieve reconciliation</u> (with temporary timeouts as needed)

The DESK system for Difficult Conversations and Conflict Resolution focuses on the observable details of the trespass and how both the sufferer and the trespasser can cooperatively reconcile the trespass.

<u>Note</u>: the focus is on the observable details of the trespass incident and not on the character of any individual. When DESK was explained to me, it was described as a system from the sufferer's perspective only, but it also works from the trespasser's perspective.

I have clarified the steps and embellished the system that was presented to me. I have enhanced the *describe* step of the DESK process. I include Albert Mehrabian's 7-38-55 Rule of Personal Communication (from the sufferer's perspective). I have added an additional step, which includes active listening (from the trespasser's perspective).

The sufferer commonly escalates the experience to conflict by using criticism or complaint, to which the trespasser will usually respond with defensiveness. Criticism and defensiveness are two sides of the same pride coin, so it makes sense to me that DESK can be used in both directions.

I also suggest that the DESK process be ended with a brainstorming session to develop solutions to prevent the trespass from recurring. Instead of complaining at or about your spouse, you should DESKribe to your spouse.

I was introduced to the DESK system for Difficult Conversations and Conflict Resolution when I started talking with a counsellor in the early 1990s to help me deal with issues from my *biological* family of origin and my divorce.

Marriage with a Crazy-Maker-Manipulator was often grand. When my ex-wife turned her wiles on me, life was euphoric. However, after many years of her addiction to spending and gambling, her manipulations became empty. She had an expression that she often said to me: "What's mine is mine, and what's yours is mine."

I must be honest and admit that I was not innocent in the demise of my first marriage. The dark, defensive side of RATS has an allure of vengeance that seems justifiable at the time. However, the continual emoting of any negative emotions always leads to becoming a RATS. At the time of my divorce, I was a primary Relationship RATS-Conformer and a primary Technical RATS-Hypercritic. Instead of using my knowledge to help, I used my knowledge for revenge and flipped from positive STAR to negative RATS.

When I separated our bank accounts to protect my family's finances from my ex-wife's spending and gambling addictions, she left me, our family home, and our children to live with her boyfriend.

When she later asked to come back into my home, I made counselling sessions a prerequisite before I would allow her back into our family home. The counsellor asked my ex-wife and me to take turns using the DESK approach to address any incident (from the sufferer's perspective). The counsellor asked me to go first, and I completed the process within fifteen minutes with some guidance.

After two one-hour sessions with the counsellor, my ex-wife could not successfully use the DESK process. She demanded that I accept her back <u>without counselling</u>, and I refused. So, she decided that she preferred divorce over learning a new skill. She then promised to use her knowledge as a divorce lawyer's assistant to destroy me if I did not allow her back home without counselling.

I have found that the DESK system works very well as long as everyone involved in the conflict is committed to the process. The trespasser is not allowed to speak until the sufferer has finished speaking everything they desire to say. This strategy forces the trespasser to listen to all of the details before speaking.

I believe that the DESK approach works for all difficult relationships as long as both sides cooperate. I believe that the relationships between governments and their citizens could benefit significantly from the open and honest communications that DESK can facilitate, especially concerning government-led racism, breaches of trust, and other ungodly legislation and actions.

DESK from the Holy Bible

Before I explain the DESK process, it is helpful to study the approach that Paul demonstrated in the Holy Bible:

Romans 1:7-8 (KJV) To all that be in Rome, beloved of God, called to be saints: Grace to you and peace from God our Father, and the Lord Jesus Christ. First, I thank my God through Jesus Christ for you all, that your faith is spoken of throughout the whole world.

Romans 1:17 (KJV) For therein is the righteousness of God revealed from faith to faith: as it is written, The just shall live by faith.

Psalm 46:1 & 48:14 & 2 Corinthians 12:9 (KJV) God is our refuge and strength, a very present help in trouble. For this God is our God for ever and ever: he will be our guide even unto death. And he said unto me, My grace is sufficient for thee: for my strength is made perfect in weakness. Most gladly therefore will I rather glory in my infirmities, that the power of Christ may rest upon me.

Start the DESK process with praise for what is important within the relationship. Starting with praise will set the mood for the speaker as well as the listener. I also suggest a prayer to invite God into the conversation. God's Presence will ensure that the sufferer can calmly express their feelings with attention to Albert Mehrabian's 7-38-55 Rule of Personal Communication. God's Presence will also ensure that the trespasser can calmly receive the words without any preconceived judgment, paying attention to active listening and incorporating reflective and empathic listening.

Romans 2:1 (KJV) Therefore thou art inexcusable, O man, whosoever thou art that judgest: for wherein thou judgest another, thou condemnest thyself; for thou that judgest doest the same things.

Paul has a primary Action Personality Style, and he quickly gets to the point in a straightforward approach, stating the trespass, the needed correction, and the rebuke.

I suggest using the DESK approach at this point instead of the direct rebuke. The trespasser might better receive the DESK approach rather than Paul's approach of a direct accusation.

Romans 16:19-20 (KJV) For your obedience is come abroad unto all men. I am glad therefore on your behalf: but yet I would have you wise unto that which is good, and simple concerning evil. And the God of peace shall bruise Satan under your feet shortly. The grace of our Lord Jesus Christ be with you. Amen.

Finish the DESK process with words of encouragement. Everyone interested in love, joy, peace, and harmony in their relationships needs to see that the end goal is within reach.

After both the sufferer and trespasser have had an opportunity to use DESK to communicate, there is still the issue of atonement in finding acceptable ways to prevent the recurrence of the trespass. Wait for the brainstorming session (after the

DESKribing sessions are completed) to discuss solutions. Proposing solutions in the DESKribing sessions could result in escalated conflict and walkaway timeouts.

DESK Scenarios

I will use two scenarios to describe the DESK process briefly. The names in the scenarios are conveniently Dad, Mom and Children. These two scenarios are fictional but help to demonstrate the DESK process:

Scenario One:
The family has had a hectic week, and it is now Sunday afternoon. The family has decided to go on a family picnic. The forecast is for a warm, cloudy day. Mom is inside the house preparing and packing food for the picnic, while Dad is outside collecting and loading the toys, chairs, picnic blankets, magazines, etc.

The family packed themselves into the car for this day trip and drove one hour to a picnic area near a local beach. When they arrived at the picnic area, Dad unpacked the toys, games, and the cooler with the food. Dad played with the children while Mom laid out the picnic blanket and set out the food.

A rainstorm suddenly and unexpectedly drenched the picnic blanket and food. Mom is furious at Dad, who is a lot of fun for the children but almost always fails to plan for details and almost always forgets important things, for example, forgetting to pack the day tent or bring umbrellas to protect them from today's rainstorm.

Dad (the trespasser) had failed to prepare for the rainstorm, and everything Mom (the sufferer) prepared for the picnic was ruined.

Scenario Two:
The family has had a hectic week, and it is now Sunday morning. Mom woke up early and decided to prepare a lavish break-

fast of bacon, eggs, and toast for the entire family, who was still sleeping.

The toaster was an older toaster from Mom's childhood (with sentimental value) and could only toast two slices of bread at a time; the toast pops up when the toast is ready. Mom had already toasted several slices of toast and was cooking the bacon and eggs.

While Mom's focus was on the bacon and eggs, flames started coming out of the toaster. Mom quickly put out the fire, but the smoke triggered the home's fire alarm and the smell of fire spread through the house very quickly.

Dad (the sufferer) ran into the kitchen, angry at Mom (the trespasser) for keeping what Dad considered junk and not using the new toaster oven that was sitting right beside the ancient toaster.

DESK and the Sufferer

DESK Explained from the Perspective of the Sufferer:

Imagine yourself sitting in your favourite restaurant, having a work lunch. You are doing your best to resolve a misunderstanding with your <u>best</u> *vendor,* who provides you with ninety-five percent of your hard-to-find treasures.

Everyone knows you, and the place is crowded, so you would like to avoid making a loud, angry display. Remember that your feelings are your feelings and are almost <u>never</u> wrong. However, responding with a negative emotion like anger is almost <u>always</u> wrong.

Don't focus on any other individual involved in the conflict. Instead, with all individuals facing the same direction, set an object, such as a burning candle, in front of everyone and focus on the object as the source of conflict. You are united and focused on the challenging experience.

If there is any possibility of escalation, *then* it is best to sit beside each other and focus in the same direction on something that is on the table. *If* there is an escalation, *then* it is crucial to walk away for a timeout. You need to be united and focused against the problem. *If* it is possible to maintain a calm discussion, *then* turn to sit facing each other and look into each other's eyes while speaking or listening.

On a personal note, when I was going through my divorce, my ex-wife, with the knowledge, approval, and aid of the gender-prejudiced Family Court, used my children as weapons to hurt me. My children were too young to comprehend how doing the things their mother told them to do at my home and saying the things their mother told them to say to me were causing me tremendous emotional pain.

Looking at my children while I was processing my emotional pain was like looking at instruments of torture. I have never stopped loving my children, but my emotional pain tainted my love for them. I often spoke angry words and shouted my frustrations, followed by regrets and apologies.

Over the next eleven years, I was dragged back into divorce court by an ex-wife who used her knowledge as a divorce lawyer's assistant within the gender-discriminatory Family Court system to harm me. During that time, I repeatedly needed to ask my children for their forgiveness for my frustrated behaviour.

I learned an important truth. Do not look into the eyes of someone you love when you are processing emotional pain. Do not look into the eyes of the one you are attempting to reconcile with while describing your pain until you can speak without negative emotion. While describing, externalizing and processing your pain, the sight of the individual(s) you are looking at becomes neurologically linked with your pain.

When using the DESK system, speaking from a 'keyword list' of points to be discussed is acceptable. The keyword list should only be for one issue, incident or experience, even if the trespass experience spanned multiple days. The purpose of the list is to serve as a reminder only. This list should only have one or two words for each item. Do not include any accusations or defamatory comments on the list; the list will later be shared with the trespasser to be used for their responses.

I recommend always using a keyword list. This way, the trespasser will not need to keep a record of each point discussed. The trespasser should focus on listening only and never focus on responses.

After the issue has been discussed and resolved, you do not want to bring up another issue or point that you had forgotten; it might erase the progress made during the DESK process.

Do not allow scope creep by either the sufferer or trespasser. Adding other issues to the current issue will turn the mole-hill into a mountain. If either the sufferer or the trespasser feels it is necessary to raise another issue, schedule another DESK session for a later date.

D   *DESKribe (Describe) the <u>Observable</u> <u>Facts</u> of the Incident*

'Just the Facts, ma'am/sir. Just the Facts.' <u>Never use</u> the word *You* and <u>never criticize</u>. <u>Never</u> assign *blame* or make *judgments*.

Focus on Albert Mehrabian's 7-38-55 Rule of Personal Communication. Pay attention to your facial expression, your body language, the tone and quality of your voice, and the words that you use.

Using inflammatory words like *always* and *never* are almost <u>always</u> wrong and almost <u>never</u> appropriate in a conflict situation. Another word that should be avoided is 'Why.' Why contains a metamessage that presupposes a fact to be true and usually triggers defensiveness in the receiver of the question.

For example, if I asked you, "Why did you kill your father," the metamessage is that I am one hundred percent certain that you killed your father. My presupposition will likely trigger defensiveness in you, causing you to make claims to prove that my presumption is wrong.

While the sufferer is speaking, the trespasser should use active listening skills.

Scenario (using the details previously described):
1.   Picnic scenario (Mom speaking):

<u>Preamble</u>
Mom really would like to yell: "You always forget to think about the details, and it always destroys my plans." Instead, Mom focuses on DESKribing and says in a gentle tone:
- "I planned and worked really hard to ensure that we had everything that we could possibly desire for lunch."
- "The rain came down hard for at least fifteen minutes."
- "Now our lunch is wet and soggy."

2. Breakfast scenario (Dad speaking):

<u>Preamble</u>
Dad really would like to yell: "You always collect and use junk and one day, you are going to burn the house down." Instead, Dad focuses on DESKribing and says in a gentle tone:
- "I woke up suddenly when I smelled smoke."
- "I looked for you but couldn't find you."
- "I came downstairs and found the kitchen was filled with smoke."

E   ***Express <u>Your</u> <u>Feelings</u> With "I Feel …" Statements***
Every sentence must be about you and your feelings. <u>Never use</u> the word *You* and <u>Never criticize.</u> <u>Never</u> assign *blame* or make *judgments*).

Scenario:
1. Picnic scenario (Mom speaking):
   - "<u>*I*</u> *feel disappointed* that the rain wasted all my planning and efforts."
   - "<u>*I*</u> *feel sad* that we must cut our picnic short to return home for lunch."
2. Breakfast scenario (Dad speaking):
   - "When I smelled smoke, <u>*I*</u> *felt terrified*."

S   ***Be Specific***

Stick to the scope of the conflict to be resolved. Do not allow scope creep.

Scenario:

1. Picnic scenario (Mom speaking):

    <u>Preamble</u>

    Dad almost always fails to plan for details and almost always forgets important things. Many incidents from the past could be brought forward to today to attack Dad's character flaws. Instead, Mom focuses on DESKribing and says in a gentle tone:

    - "The rain soaked everything, and I have nothing left for lunch."
    - "It is too bad that we didn't bring the day tent or umbrellas today."

2. Breakfast scenario (Dad speaking):

    <u>Preamble</u>

    Mom is always collecting what Dad considers junk. Dad can easily come up with a long list of many things around the house that do not function properly. Instead, Dad focuses on DESKribing and says in a gentle tone:

    - "This morning, when I smelled smoke and couldn't find you, I was worried about you and a possible house fire."
    - "When I came out of the bedroom and saw all the smoke, I panicked that something might have happened to you."

K   ***Keep at It Until the Conflict is <u>Calmly</u> Resolved***

Take a timeout to cool down if emotions get too hot or the *Expression* step gets derailed. Focus only on the facts and never on the other person. Remember that the issue is the behaviour only and not the person; *if* the intent was innocent, *then* the behaviour was misunderstood. Do not go to bed without kissing, hugging, or expressing your love for each other. Agree to continue again as soon as possible over the next few days if more time is needed to establish a resolution.

After the Sufferer has finished speaking, the Trespasser is given an opportunity to DESKribe from the Trespasser's perspective.

DESK and the Trespasser

DESK Explained from the Perspective of the Trespasser:

Imagine yourself sitting in your favourite restaurant, having a work lunch. You are doing your best to resolve a misunderstanding with your <u>best</u> *customer,* who purchases ninety-five percent of your hard-to-sell treasures.

Everyone knows you, and the place is packed, so you would like to avoid making a loud, angry display. Remember that your customer's feelings are their feelings and are almost <u>never</u> wrong from their perspective. However, responding with a negative emotion, like anger, is almost <u>always</u> wrong.

Don't focus on any other individual involved in the conflict. Instead, with all individuals facing the same direction, set an object, such as a burning candle, in front of everyone and focus on the object as the source of the conflict. You are united and focused on the challenging experience.

If there is any possibility of escalation, *then* it is best to sit beside each other and focus in the same direction on something that is on the table. *If* there is an escalation, *then* it is crucial to walk away for a timeout. You need to be united and focused against the problem. *If* it is possible to maintain a calm discussion, *then* sit facing each other and look into each other's eyes while speaking or listening.

If the sufferer spoke from a keyword list, *then* the list should be shared with the trespasser after the sufferer has completed speaking to allow the trespasser to respond to each item on the list.

Do not allow scope creep (by either the sufferer or trespasser). Adding other issues to the current issue will turn the mole-hill into a mountain. If either the sufferer or the trespasser feels it is necessary to raise another issue, schedule another DESK session for a later date.

D   *DESKribe (Describe) the <u>Observable</u> <u>Facts</u> of the Incident*

'Just the Facts, ma'am/sir. Just the Facts.' <u>Never use</u> the word *You* and <u>never defend.</u> <u>Never</u> return *blame* or make *judgments*. After using active listening while the sufferer was speaking, it is now the trespasser's turn to *respond in the Sufferer's Primary Personality Style.*

Focus on Albert Mehrabian's 7-38-55 Rule of Personal Communication. Pay attention to your facial expression, your body language, the tone and quality of your voice, and the words that you use.

Using inflammatory words like *always* and never are almost <u>always</u> wrong and almost <u>never</u> appropriate in a conflict situation. Another word that should be avoided is 'Why.' Why contains a metamessage that presupposes a fact to be true and usually triggers defensiveness in the receiver of the question.

For example, if I asked you, "Why did you kill your father," the metamessage is that I am one hundred percent certain that you killed your father. My presupposition will likely trigger defensiveness in you, causing you to make claims to prove that my presumption is wrong.

Now, the roles of speaker and listener are reversed. While the trespasser is speaking, the sufferer should use active listening skills.

Scenario:

1. Picnic scenario (Dad speaking):

   <u>Preamble</u>

   While Mom was speaking, Dad nodded his head and looked into Mom's eyes to assure Mom that he was paying attention.

   Dad heard Mom's task-oriented STAR language: "planning," "worked," and "for lunch" and understood that she was speaking as a primary Technical STAR. He knew that Mom would like his response to focus on details and process.

- "You really did a great job planning and getting everything together for a perfect lunch."
- "That rain really came down hard. I did not consider the possibility that it would rain."
- "I was the one who packed the car with all the non-food essentials."

2. Breakfast scenario (Mom speaking):

Preamble

While Dad was speaking, Mom nodded her head and looked into Dad's eyes to assure Dad that she was paying attention.

Mom heard Dad's people-oriented STAR language: "worried" "panicked," and understood that he was speaking as a primary Relationship STAR. She knew that Dad would like her response to be focused on feelings and emotions.

- "I was focused on preparing a great surprise breakfast with everyone's favourite foods."
- "I remember how my mom used that toaster to prepare breakfasts filled with love."

E   ***Express <u>Your Feelings</u> With "I Feel ..." Statements***

Every sentence can only be about you and your feelings so, <u>Never use</u> the word *You* and <u>Never defend.</u> <u>Never</u> return *blame* or make *judgments*.

Scenario:

1. Picnic scenario (Dad speaking):
   - "<u>*I*</u> *am sorry* that I did not think to bring the day tent or umbrellas."
   - "<u>*I*</u> *love you* for being so good at planning our meals."

2. Breakfast scenario (Mom speaking):

- *"I am sorry* that I didn't pay closer attention to the toaster."
- *"I am sorry* that I worried you."
- *"I love you* for caring so much about me and my safety."

S   ***Be Specific***

Stick to the scope of the conflict to be resolved. Do not allow scope creep.

Scenario:

1. Picnic scenario (Dad speaking):
   - "What can I do to compensate for your disappointment <u>today</u>?"
2. Breakfast scenario (Mom speaking):
   - "How can I make up for worrying you <u>this morning</u>?"

K   ***Keep at It Until the Conflict is <u>Calmly</u> Resolved.***

Take a timeout to cool down if emotions get too hot or the *Expression* gets derailed. Focus only on the facts and never on the other person. Remember that the issue is the behaviour only and not the person; *if* the intent was innocent, *then* the behaviour was misunderstood. Do not go to bed without kissing, hugging, or expressing your love for each other. Agree to continue again as soon as possible over the next few days if more time is needed to establish a resolution.

DESK Brainstorming

All the rules for DESK '7-38-55 rule of personal communication' and 'active listening' apply to everyone in this brainstorming step.

After the scope and the challenge have been defined by D, E, S, and K and agreed to by both Mom and Dad, now Mom, Dad, and Children can sit together, facing each other, and brainstorm solutions. In brainstorming sessions, no idea is to be judged. Because I am a primary Relationship STAR, I like to throw out one or two wacky ideas that bring laughter to the family.

1. Picnic scenario (brainstorming ideas):
    - Install a 64Gb Memory stick implant into Dad's brain☺
    - Make a checklist of games and toys
    - Make a checklist of food items and accessories
    - Make a checklist of emergency items
    - Bring money to go to a restaurant – just in case
    - Organize a pre-trip planning meeting to discuss:
        - The trip objective for each member of the family
        - Any special friend, game, or toy to bring along
        - Potential Problem Solutions
2. Breakfast scenario (brainstorming ideas):
    - Make sure that the Fire Department is onsite when using junk equipment☺
    - Make a quality control checklist for all items brought home that were previously used.

21. RATS, Grow Up Or Be Left Behind

People have been blaming others for their own wickedness since Adam and Eve. Adam blamed God for creating Eve. Adam blamed Eve for giving Adam the forbidden fruit. Eve blamed the snake (Satan) for deceiving Eve.

Neither Adam nor Eve took ownership of their sin. Neither Adam nor Eve repented of their sin. Both Adam and Eve paid the atonement cost of their Sin-Debt.

Do not justify your wickedness by blaming your wicked parents, spouse, society, nation, or government. You are the only one responsible for your righteousness or wickedness.

Ezekiel was a priest and a prophet living in slavery. God had punished the nation of Judah for generations of wickedness (unrepented sin). God allowed the people of Judah to be enslaved by Babylon as atonement for their wickedness.

Ezekiel was enslaved with the wicked people of Judah to be their priest. Many of the people repented of their wickedness. While in Slavery, God called Ezekiel to be a Prophet.

> *Ezekiel 18:1-2 (KJV) The word of the LORD came unto me again, saying, What mean ye, that ye use this proverb concerning the land of Israel, saying, The fathers have eaten sour grapes, and the children's teeth are set on edge?*

In Ezekiel 18:1-2, we read that the people of Judah, who lived in Babylon as slaves, blamed their circumstances on their ancestors. While this is correct, this mindset avoids their responsibility to behave righteously and prevents the possibility of repentance. They also justified their Sin-Nature and current iniquity by blaming their ancestors.

To explain why and how RATS must grow up, I will use the common experience of mothers or fathers from our Physical World.

However, you can only grow up in the Spiritual World by connecting and developing your own personal and direct relationship with the Triune God (Almighty-God-Jehovah, Holy Spirit, and Jesus Christ). There will be some people who can help you *start* your Spiritual Journey, but you must grow *on your own* within your Kingdom Family. The Holy Trinity will be your Kingdom Family and will guide your Spiritual Mind, Heart, and Will from Crazy-Maker to RATS and STAR.

It is also important to remember that every Saint is either a son or daughter of God. God has no grandsons or granddaughters. From God's perspective, we are all sons or daughters of God. In the Kingdom of Heaven, your father will be your brother, and your mother will be your sister.

Ezekiel 18:3-9 (KJV) As I live, saith the Lord GOD, ye shall not have occasion any more to use this proverb in Israel. Behold, all souls are mine; as the soul of the father, so also the soul of the son is mine: the soul that sinneth, it shall die. But if a man be just, and do that which is lawful and right, And hath not eaten upon the mountains, neither hath lifted up his eyes to the idols of the house of Israel, neither hath defiled his neighbour's wife, neither hath come near to a menstruous woman, And hath not oppressed any, but hath restored to the debtor his pledge, hath spoiled none by violence, hath given his bread to the hungry, and hath covered the naked with a garment; He that hath not given forth upon usury, neither hath taken any increase, that hath withdrawn his hand from iniquity, hath executed true judgment between man and man, Hath walked in my statutes, and hath kept my judgments, to deal truly; he is just, he shall surely live, saith the Lord GOD.

In Ezekiel 18:3-9, God tells the people to stop blaming their current sinfulness on their ancestors.

Any parent will probably recognize this type of behaviour. One child blames their bad behaviour on their brother, saying, "But he started it!"

As parents in this physical world, we know that we need to stop the bad behaviour of the one who started the conflict. And we need to stop the bad behaviour of the one who retaliated. If parents were not already aware, they probably quickly learned that retaliation leads to escalation of disagreement to conflict and ultimately to violence.

Ezekiel 18:10-13 (KJV) If he beget a son that is a robber, a shedder of blood, and that doeth the like to any one of these things, And that doeth not any of those duties, but even hath eaten upon the mountains, and defiled his neighbour's wife, Hath oppressed the poor and needy, hath spoiled by violence, hath not restored the pledge, and hath lifted up his eyes to the idols, hath committed abomination, Hath given forth upon usury, and hath taken increase: shall he then live? he shall not live: he hath done all these abominations; he shall surely die; his blood shall be upon him.

In Ezekiel 18:10-13, God explains to the people that God will not punish a righteous father for the sins of his wicked son.

Parents, in this physical world, comprehend that punishing the righteous son or daughter for the actions of a naughty son or daughter will ultimately cause the righteous son or daughter to become naughty in rebellion against injustice.

Ezekiel 18:14-17 (KJV) Now, lo, if he beget a son, that seeth all his father's sins which he hath done, and considereth, and doeth not such like, That hath not eaten upon the mountains, neither hath lifted up his eyes to the idols of the house of Israel, hath not defiled his neighbour's wife, Neither hath oppressed any, hath not withholden the pledge, neither hath spoiled by violence, but hath given his bread to the hungry, and hath covered the naked with a garment, That hath taken off his hand from the poor, that hath not received usury nor increase, hath executed my judgments, hath walked in my statutes; he shall not die for the iniquity of his father, he shall surely live.

In Ezekiel 18:14-17, God tells the people that God will not punish a righteous son for the sins of his wicked father.

Again, parents comprehend that punishing the righteous son or daughter for the actions of a naughty son or daughter will ultimately cause the righteous son or daughter to become naughty in rebellion against injustice.

Ezekiel 18:18-19 (KJV) As for his father, because he cruelly oppressed, spoiled his brother by violence, and did that which is not good among his people, lo, even he shall die in his iniquity. Yet say ye, Why? doth not the son bear the iniquity of the father? When the son hath done that which is lawful and right, and hath kept all my statutes, and hath done them, he shall surely live.

The concept of avoiding blaming others is important enough that, in Ezekiel 18:18-19, God repeats that sons cannot justify their iniquity by blaming their fathers.

Ezekiel 18:20-22 (KJV) The soul that sinneth, it shall die. The son shall not bear the iniquity of the father, neither shall the father bear the iniquity of the son: the righteousness of the righteous shall be upon him, and the wickedness of the wicked shall be upon him. But if the wicked will turn from all his sins that he hath committed, and keep all my statutes, and do that which is lawful and right, he shall surely live, he shall not die. All his transgressions that he hath committed, they shall not be mentioned unto him: in his righteousness that he hath done he shall live.

The soul that sins shall suffer (spiritually die) only for their own sins.

Ezekiel 18:23-24 (KJV) Have I any pleasure at all that the wicked should die? saith the Lord GOD: and not that he should return from his ways, and live? But when the righteous turneth away from his righteousness, and committeth iniquity, and doeth according to all the abominations that the wicked man doeth, shall he live? All his righteousness that he hath done shall not be mentioned: in his trespass that he hath trespassed, and in his sin that he hath sinned, in them shall he die.

God does not enjoy the death of any wicked man, woman, boy or girl. When anyone righteous knowingly chooses to become wicked by rejecting God, they will suffer when they spiritually die.

Most parents prefer that their sons and daughters get along harmoniously with their siblings. No parent enjoys being forced to intervene in children's squabbles.

Ezekiel 18:25-26 (KJV) Yet ye say, The way of the Lord is not equal [fair]. Hear now, O house of Israel; Is not my way equal [fair]? are not your ways unequal [unfair]? When a righteous man turneth away from his righteousness, and committeth iniquity, and dieth in them; for his iniquity that he hath done shall he die. [Clarification term added]

Do not accuse God of being unfair when the righteous knowingly choose to become wicked and suffer for their wickedness.

It is probably rare that any parent has not experienced a typical good son or daughter misbehaving and accusing the mother or father of being unfair when disciplined for their bad behaviour.

Ezekiel 18:27-28 (KJV) Again, when the wicked man turneth away from his wickedness that he hath committed, and doeth that which is lawful and right, he shall save his soul alive. Because he considereth, and turneth away from all his transgressions that he hath committed, he shall surely live, he shall not die.

Ezekiel 18:27-28: When the wicked choose to repent and become righteous to escape their suffering, the righteous will continue to suffer until they have paid their Sin-Debt, but will have saved their spirit from spiritual death.

Every parent hopes that disciplining the misbehaving son or daughter will result in good behaviour until the end of time.

Ezekiel 18:29-30 (KJV) Yet saith the house of Israel, The way of the Lord is not equal. O house of Israel, are not my ways equal? are not your ways unequal? Therefore I will judge you, O house of Israel, every one according to his ways, saith the

Lord GOD. Repent, and turn yourselves from all your transgressions; so iniquity shall not be your ruin.

Ezekiel 18:29-30: God judges you and allows you to suffer because of your iniquity (unrepented sin).

When a son or daughter willfully misbehaves, disciplinary action (lecture, timeout, grounding, etc.) is usually needed to prevent a repeat of the misbehaviour.

Ezekiel 18:31 (KJV) Cast away from you all your transgressions, whereby ye have transgressed; and make you a new heart and a new spirit: for why will ye die, O house of Israel?

If you are wicked, repent, and become righteous, God will welcome you back.

Every parent hopes that one episode of disciplinary correction will guarantee good behaviour until the end of time.

Ezekiel 18:32 (KJV) For I have no pleasure in the death of him that dieth, saith the Lord GOD: wherefore turn yourselves, and live ye.

This concept was important enough that God repeated this message for a third time in this chapter. God does not enjoy the death of any wicked man, woman, boy or girl.

If you see something wrong in the world, you can either do nothing or you can do something to correct the wrong. If you see something wrong in yourself, you can either do nothing or you can do something to correct the wrong. If you see something wrong in someone else, you cannot do anything except protect yourself.

John 6:64 (KJV) But there are some of you that believe not. For Jesus knew from the beginning who they were that believed not, and who should betray him.

Mark 14:43-44 (KJV) And immediately, while he yet spake, cometh Judas, one of the twelve, and with him a great multitude with swords and staves, from the chief priests and

Throughout the Holy Bible, God chose the most unlikely people to become heroes. They only needed to trust God and take the first step. Jesus created a team of apostles out of men who were not highly respected.

Paul was a zealot with an Action Personality Style. Thomas was a thinker with a Technical Personality Style. John was Jesus' favourite with a Relationship Personality Style. Judas Iscariot had a negative-melodramatic Support Personality Style.

It might seem odd to include Judas Iscariot, the traitor, as a Support Personality Style, but he asked that the chief priests 'lead Jesus away safely.' We don't know what was in Judas' mind. It might be that Judas actually believed that Jesus was the rightful king and believed that Jesus needed a push to start the revolt to take his rightful place as king.

If Judas believed Jesus was the rightful king, *then* Judas might also have believed that God would rescue Jesus and install Jesus as King of the Jews. After Jesus was arrested and tortured, it became obvious that God would not rescue Jesus and that Jesus would not become a worldly king. Judas regretted his actions and committed suicide.

There were no great Christian orators until Paul. Jesus taught his team, and they became a team of tremendous influencers. The number of Jesus' followers grew from twelve to millions, or billions, worldwide. I believe that you need Jesus and his doctrine on your team to become your best.

The Holy Bible teaches us to avoid being conformed to Man's World and keep our spiritual growth focused on God.

Growing up to become a Kingdom of Heaven STAR is always simple, but it is also never easy. It is simple because all you have to do is follow Jesus and do what he does. It is not easy because there are many stumbling blocks along the journey.

Jesus already showed us the path around the stumbling blocks, but the path is narrow and winding, and we cannot know the path unless we study the entire Holy Bible. Most people stop when they find a wide path that is both straight and easy. Along the wide path, the seven pillars of society (banks, government, medicine, education, entertainment, religion, and family) will make your decisions and decide your direction for you.

I do not treat Technology as a separate pillar because each of the other pillars uses Technology. The seven pillars of society, especially with the use of Technology, distract God's Children away from God's Teachings.

2 Corinthians 7:10-11 (KJV) For godly sorrow worketh repentance to salvation not to be repented of: but the sorrow of the world worketh death. For behold this selfsame thing, that ye sorrowed after a godly sort, what carefulness it wrought in you, yea, what clearing of yourselves, yea, what indignation, yea, what fear, yea, what vehement desire, yea, what zeal, yea, what revenge! In all things ye have approved yourselves to be clear in this matter.

The Holy Bible teaches that godly sorrow based on righteousness saves, while worldly sorrow based on pride kills. A trespasser's first natural reaction is to relieve their guilt or shame by defending their bad behaviour.

Pride prevents the trespasser from saying, "I am wrong, and I am sorry." Remember that an apology must be timely and specific. If the trespasser makes a general apology long after irreparable harm, it is ineffective because the poisonous words have already damaged the sufferer's Spiritual Mind and Heart.

Don't allow the sin of pride to enter into your Spiritual Mind or Heart. When you compare yourself against someone else and see yourself as better than they are, this is a sin rooted in pride. When you rejoice, take comfort, or feel pleasure in someone's mistake or failure, this is a sin rooted in pride.

James 1:13-15 (KJV) Let no man say when he is tempted, I am tempted of God: for God cannot be tempted with evil, neither tempteth he any man: But every man is tempted, when he is drawn away of his own lust, and enticed. Then when lust hath conceived, it bringeth forth sin: and sin, when it is finished, bringeth forth death.

The Holy Bible also teaches that living a truly godly life is joyful and fulfilling. This lesson does not mean living a life of lack, and it does not mean removing joy from life.

Imagine a father who tells his son to keep away from a hot stove. But the boy really wants some treasure from the back of the stove and decides to ignore his father, so he touches the hot stove anyway.

The boy failed to reach the treasure and suffered a painful burn.

The father had told the boy to avoid the hot stove to keep him safe and not deprive him of the joy of holding his treasure. The boy would have enjoyed his treasure without the burn if he had asked his father for help.

In the same way, God gives us rules to keep us safe from Satan and not to deprive us of joy.

2 Corinthians 10:12 (KJV) For we dare not make ourselves of the number, or compare ourselves with some that commend themselves: but they measuring themselves by themselves, and comparing themselves among themselves, are not wise.

2 Corinthians 10:12 teaches that everyone is unique and we should not compare ourselves with others in the world.

When you compare yourself against someone else and desire what they have, this is a sin rooted in pride. When you judge someone else, this is a sin rooted in pride. There will always be someone better than you in some aspect of your life, but there will always be some aspect of your life that is better than 'someone else.'

Many claim phenomenal spiritual experiences, gifts, and abilities. However, do not become discouraged if you do not have the same gifts and abilities that they have. God gave you the talents that you need for your Kingdom Assignment; therefore, you are already perfect. Accept your skillset as perfect for you; accept their skillset as perfect for them.

God described David as "a man after my heart," so it is clear that God highly regarded David. However, David was not considered a prophet because he did not see the future in visions, perform miracles, or communicate directly with God, as did other Prophets named in the Holy Bible.

1 Peter 4:10 (KJV) As every man hath received the gift, even so minister the same one to another, as good stewards of the manifold grace of God.

Titus 3:14 (KJV) … learn to maintain good works for necessary uses, that they be not unfruitful.

Colossians 3:23-24 (KJV) And whatsoever ye do, do it heartily, as to the Lord, and not unto men; Knowing that of the Lord ye shall receive the reward of the inheritance: for ye serve the Lord Christ.

*Ephesians 4:6-7 & 11-16 (KJV) (KJV) One God and Father of all, who is above all, and through all, and in you all. But unto every one of us is given grace according to the measure of the gift of Christ. **And he gave some, apostles; and some, prophets; and some, evangelists; and some, pastors and teachers**; For the perfecting of the saints, for the work of the ministry, for the edifying of the body of Christ: Till we all come in the unity of the faith, and of the knowledge of the Son of God, unto a perfect man, unto the measure of the stature of the fulness of Christ: That we henceforth be no more children, tossed to and fro, and carried about with every wind of* *doctrine, by the sleight of men, and cunning craftiness, whereby they lie in wait to deceive; But speaking the truth in love, may grow up into him in all things, which is the head, even Christ: From whom the whole body fitly joined together and compacted by that which every joint supplieth, according to the effectual working in the measure of every part, maketh increase of the body unto the edifying of itself in love. [Emphasis added]*

You were created perfectly equipped for your Kingdom Assignment, and everyone else was created perfectly equipped for their Kingdom Assignment.

Someone coming to work with a carload of camping equipment would not be well equipped for working as an accountant, just as someone equipped only with pencil, paper, eraser, stapler, and calculator would not be well equipped to spend a week in the wilderness.

Don't measure yourself against the gifts of others. Don't measure others against your gifts. Get on with your Kingdom Assignment. Remember that God loves you exactly as you are. You would still love your son or daughter if they did not win the gold medal in the Olympics, and God still loves you if you do not accomplish your Kingdom Assignment. Remember that God loves everyone else even if they do not accomplish their Kingdom Assignment.

I have a Hindu friend who is strongly spiritual in his faith. We would often talk neutrally for hours about our respective spiritual views. I do not try to convert him, nor does he try to convert me.

One day, while I was discussing spirituality with my friend, he told me a fascinating Hindu parable. I don't know the story word for word, as told to me, so I am going to paraphrase it here.

A very devout man had been praying fervently, each day, for many years for the blessing of children. His neighbour made no time for anything spiritual but had many children, and the devout man envied his neighbour.

One day, God appeared to the man and said, "I would like you to fill a glass full to the brim with water and carry the water around the house three times without spilling a drop."

The devout man filled a glass full of water. Because this was an assignment from God, the devout man diligently focused on the rim of the glass as he carried the glass of water around the house.

The devout man completed walking around the house three times without spilling a drop and stopped triumphantly in front of God.

God said to the man, "I did not hear you pray to me even once during your walk with the glass of water."

The man defended himself by saying, "But I was so focused on the task you assigned for me to walk around the house without spilling a drop that I could not pray."

Then God said to the man, "Your neighbour's task is to raise children, and he is so focused on his task that he does not have time to pray. Your task is to pray, and you should be so focused on your task that you do not have time to raise children."

Everyone should focus on completing their assigned task to the best of their abilities and leave everyone else to do the same with their assigned tasks.

John 14:6 (KJV) Jesus saith unto him, I am the way, the truth, and the life: no man cometh unto the Father, but by me.

John 8:12 (KJV) Then spake Jesus again unto them, saying, I am the light of the world: he that followeth me shall not walk in darkness, but shall have the light of life.

Matthew 5:14-16 (KJV) Ye are the light of the world. A city that is set on an hill cannot be hid. Neither do men light a candle, and put it under a bushel, but on a candlestick; and it giveth light unto all that are in the house. Let your light so shine before men, that they may see your good works, and glorify your Father which is in heaven.

Jesus is the way, the truth, the life, and the light. Jesus is a Kingdom of Heaven STAR, and Jesus has now charged each of us with the duty and power to be lights to the world by being in His likeness. to become a Kingdom of Heaven STAR as he is a Kingdom of Heaven STAR.

> *Acts 10:28 (KJV) And he said unto them, Ye know how that **it is an unlawful thing for a man that is a Jew to keep company, or come unto one of another nation**; but God hath shewed me that I should not call any man common or unclean. [Emphasis Added]*

> *John 10:30-32 (KJV) I and my Father are one. **Then the Jews took up stones again to stone him**. Jesus answered them, Many good works have I shewed you from my Father; for which of those works do ye stone me? [Emphasis Added]*

Matthew 27:1 and John 10:30-32 describe the Pharisees, scribes, chief priests, and elders as willing to sentence someone to death to protect their religion and laws.

> *Galatians 3:28 (KJV) **There is neither Jew nor Greek, there is neither bond nor free, there is neither male nor female: for ye are all one in Christ Jesus**. [Emphasis Added]*

> *Genesis 1:27 (KJV) So God created man in his own image, in the image of God created he him; male and female created he them.*

> *Numbers 23:19 (KJV) God is not a man, … neither the son of man, …John 4:24 (KJV) God is a Spirit: and they that worship him must worship him in spirit and in truth.*

> *John 4:7,9 (KJV) There cometh a woman of Samaria to draw water: Jesus saith unto her, Give me to drink. Then saith the woman of Samaria unto him, How is it that thou, being a Jew, askest drink of me, which am a woman of Samaria? for the Jews have no dealings with the Samaritans.*

The Holy Bible teaches us that we are created in God's Image and that God is not a man; God is a spirit.

If God is a spirit and is not a man and therefore does not have a body, we cannot judge each other based on physical differences. Racism and prejudice did not come from the teachings of the Holy Bible; Jesus chastised the Pharisees for their teaching of man's laws as being more important than God's Laws.

Based on man's laws in Israel, accepting anything from Samaritans or heathens was considered a crime, but Jesus ignored man's rules and remained obedient to God's Laws.

Based on man-made prejudices in Israel, men were discouraged from interacting with women, but Jesus ignored the prejudice. Based on man's laws in Israel, the righteous were not permitted to speak with women or sinners. Jesus socialized with an adulteress. This sin was considered one of the worst sins and was punishable by stoning to death. Jesus ignored these prejudices to show the way, to be the truth, the life and the light.

Matthew 8:5-10 (KJV) And when Jesus was entered into Capernaum, there came unto him a centurion, beseeching him, And saying, Lord, my servant lieth at home sick of the palsy, grievously tormented. And Jesus saith unto him, I will come and heal him. The centurion answered and said, Lord, I am not worthy that thou shouldest come under my roof: but speak the word only, and my servant shall be healed. For I am a man under authority, having soldiers under me: and I say to this man, Go, and he goeth; and to another, Come, and he cometh; and to my servant, Do this, and he doeth it. When Jesus heard it, he marvelled, and said to them that followed, Verily I say unto you, I have not found so great faith, no, not in Israel.

*Acts 10:28 (KJV) And he said unto them, Ye know how that **it is an unlawful thing for a man that is a Jew to keep company, or come unto one of another nation**; but God hath shewed me that I should not call any man common or unclean. [Emphasis Added]*

Based on man's laws in Israel, Jews were not allowed to speak with Gentiles. The centurion was a Roman and, therefore, a Gentile. Not only did Jesus ignore the legislated prejudice, but he further violated the law by praising the Gentiles as having a stronger faith than any Jew in Israel.

Jesus is the way, the truth, the life, and the light, and he repeatedly instructed his followers to be obedient to God over obedience to Man.

If you are a RATS or Crazy-Maker, you need to grow up or be left behind. No counsellor can do this for you; this is a journey that you need to undertake for yourself. Counsellors can only help you prepare for the growth to the higher stages of STAR. Jesus is the way, and only Jesus can show you the way to become a Kingdom of Heaven STAR and how to manifest the spiritual Kingdom of Heaven on Earth into your life.

To grow from Crazy-Maker to RATS or from RATS to STAR, everyone must take a hard, honest look at themselves, stop lying to themselves and others about their character fault(s), and take steps to behave like Jesus. Stop yelling, stop blaming, stop criticizing, stop complaining. Stop all negative emotions and negative behaviour and start behaving like a STAR. Start behaving like Jesus and follow the instructions of the Holy Bible.

Everyone will make mistakes, and everyone must accept their mistakes and resolve to do better next time.

The journey from Crazy-Maker to RATS and then to STAR is a growth journey similar to the journey from elementary school to Ph.D. Crazy-Makers and RATSs must be willing to write their own exams to graduate to the next level. As you come closer to the Ph.D. level, the tests, or tribulations, become longer in duration, more solitary, and more difficult to complete.

For example, a Ph.D. thesis must be completed by you alone and will likely take the whole school year to complete. Never give up because eternal life with Jesus is the ultimate spiritual reward. The spiritual Kingdom of Heaven on Earth is the immediate reward for those willing to make an effort now.

The new physical Kingdom of Heaven will not be available until the second coming of Jesus. However, the spiritual Kingdom of Heaven on Earth is at hand, here, now, inside you, and all around you, whenever you are ready to receive God's

Love, Peace, Joy and Happiness, and whenever you are ready to make an effort to transform yourself.

If you choose to remain a Crazy-Maker or RATS, fellow Christians will pass you by. You cannot gain your Ph.D. by sitting in the Kindergarten class, and you cannot achieve your Kingdom of Heaven STAR by sitting in the Crazy-Maker class. Do the work. Pass the tests. And rely on the Godhead to help you on your journey. With God's Help, many people have experienced immediate and complete relief from long-time addictions. With God's Help, you can do it.

*Philippians 3:12-14 (KJV) Not as though I had already attained, either were already perfect: but I follow after, if that I may apprehend that for which also I am apprehended of Christ Jesus. Brethren, I count not myself to have apprehended: but this one thing I do, **forgetting those things which are behind, and reaching forth unto those things which are before, I press toward the mark for the prize of the high calling of God in Christ Jesus**. [Emphasis added]*

The Holy Bible teaches that you cannot undo the past, so stay focused on the future starting today. Remain focused on becoming Christ-like. Crazy-Makers and RATSs must take ownership of their mistakes. Crazy-Makers and RATSs are the only ones who can control the words that come out of their mouths, and they are the only ones who can control the emotions that come out of their hearts.

I recommend that everyone read and follow the healing steps outlined in Dr. Rob Reimer's book 'Soul Care.'

People who are suffering from interaction with Crazy-Makers or RATSs should also read Dr. Rob Reimer's book 'Soul Care' because they are at risk of being dragged down to the level of RATS or Crazy-Maker.

In addition, people suffering from interaction with Crazy-Makers or RATSs should also read Gary Thomas' book 'When to Walk Away.'

2 Peter 1:3-4 (KJV) According as his divine power hath given unto us all things that pertain unto life and godliness, through the knowledge of him that hath called us to glory and virtue: Whereby are given unto us exceeding great and precious promises: that by these ye might be partakers of the divine nature, having escaped the corruption that is in the world through lust.

The Holy Bible teaches that it is through our knowledge of God and through living according to God's Glory and virtue that we will receive God's "exceeding great and precious promises." Remember that eternal life in heaven is the reward for your efforts.

Every Christian should read the Holy Bible, The Secret Message of Jesus, and Positive Personality Profiles and watch A Better Us. Dr. Charles Stanley, Pastor Andy Stanley, and Dr. David Jeremiah are excellent teachers and are available on YouTube.

Read whichever version of the Holy Bible you are most comfortable with. If you are very good with languages like I am, you might enjoy the King James Version.

Grow up or be left behind. You cannot change anyone else; you can only change yourself. *If* your partner is not willing to graduate to the higher levels of STAR with you, *then* you might need to walk away. Make an effort for your spiritual life and let others make an effort for their spiritual life. Ignore the false teachings of those who choose to profit from your spiritual immaturity. Stop being Satan's slave and start being God's Steward.

Stop, Look, and Listen when stepping into Man's World. Use godly spiritual eyes and ears. Use your free will to protect your spirit while crossing through Man's World "for we walk by faith, not by sight" (2 Corinthians 5:7). Stop obeying devils, demons, and other evil entities and principalities, and beware of evil people serving Satan.

Start focusing on God's Blessings and stop counting the likes and followers on your Facebook and Twitter accounts. Allow the Holy Spirit to help you discern evil to avoid Satan's pitfalls and traps.

Take the first baby step toward the open arms of your Godhead family – your Lord God, your Lord Holy Spirit, and your Lord Jesus Christ. The spiritual Kingdom of Heaven on Earth can be yours now if you are willing to make an effort.

Jesus is the way, the light, and the life. Follow Jesus to the spiritual Kingdom of Heaven on Earth, which is at hand, here, now, inside you, and all around you if you choose to accept. Jesus is your leader. The Holy Spirit is your Guide, and God is your source of true love, joy, peace, harmony, provision, protection, and everything good.

Your choice is simple: choose Satan's pain and suffering or choose God's Joy and Blessings.

God created the earth; Man defined the world. Don't be deceived by the subliminal marketing of Satan's World. Live in God's Heaven on Earth. Stop blaming others. Stop controlling others. Start living your life according to the true word of God by following the way of Jesus. Follow Jesus' light out of the darkness of Satan's world and into God's spiritual Kingdom of Heaven on Earth. Don't make excuses. Don't procrastinate. Don't follow Satan into his pleasure pits. Don't be distracted or divided away from your leader, Jesus Christ. Don't make excuses. I like a quote that I heard from Mike Clemons, a guest speaker on A Better Us: "Excuses are like belly buttons. Everyone has one, but none of them are any good."

Choose the rewards of Satan's world or the blessings of God's spiritual Kingdom of Heaven on Earth. If you choose to sit on the fence, you will be impaled by the fence post.

Grow up or be left behind. It is never too late to choose God.

22. Overcoming RATS Syndrome

If you are a RATS or a Crazy-Maker, you are not allowed to remain a RATS or Crazy-Maker for the rest of your life. *If* you have decided that it is impossible to overcome your RATS or Crazy-Maker nature, *then* you have unknowingly declared that you revere Satan as stronger than God.

God's Desire and expectation are that we each experience tribulations as growing pains to grow up and come away from evil. Don't put your confidence in <u>your</u> ability to overcome RATS syndrome; instead, put your confidence in <u>God's</u> Ability to guide you to become a STAR. In the appendix, I have included a prayer that I often use.

*1 Corinthians 13:11, 19 (KJV) When I was a child, I spake as a child, I understood as a child, I thought as a child: but **when I became a man, I put away childish things**. [Emphasis added]*

*Ezekiel 33:10-11 (KJV) Therefore, O thou son of man, speak unto the house of Israel; Thus ye speak, saying, If our transgressions and our sins be upon us, and we pine away in them, how should we then live? Say unto them, **As I live, saith the Lord GOD, I have no pleasure in the [spiritual] death of the wicked; but that the wicked turn from his way and live: turn ye, turn ye from your evil ways**; for why will ye die, O house of Israel? But if the wicked turn from his wickedness, and do that which is lawful and right, he shall live thereby. [Clarification terms and emphasis added]*

Jeremiah 29:11 (KJV) For I know the thoughts that I think toward you, saith the LORD, thoughts of peace, and not of evil, to give you an expected end.

*2 Chronicles 7:14 (KJV) **If my people**, which are called by my name, shall humble themselves, and pray, and seek my face, and **turn from their wicked ways; then will I hear from heaven, and will forgive their sin, and will heal their land**. [Emphasis added]*

*Psalm 37:23-24 (KJV) **The steps of a good man are ordered by the LORD**: and he delighteth in his way. Though he fall, he* *shall not be utterly cast down: for **the LORD upholdeth him with his hand**. [Emphasis added]*

*Isaiah 41:10 (KJV) **Fear thou not; for I am with thee: be not dismayed; for I am thy God: I will strengthen thee; yea, I will help thee; yea, I will uphold thee with the right hand of my righteousness**. [Emphasis added]*

The Holy Bible explains that God's Thoughts toward each of us are for good and not for evil, so God will guide you to the good things that he has planned for you. Anyone can overcome the RATS or Crazy-Maker Syndrome. It is almost as simple as growing up, and with God's Help, anything is possible.

Philippians 4:8 (KJV) … whatsoever things are true, whatsoever things are honest, whatsoever things are just, whatsoever things are pure, whatsoever things are lovely, whatsoever things are of good report; if there be any virtue, and if there be any praise, think on these things.

Proverbs 3:5-6 & Isaiah 58:11 (KJV) Trust in the LORD with all thine heart; and lean not unto thine own understanding. In all thy ways acknowledge him, and he shall direct thy paths. And the LORD shall guide thee continually, … .

The Holy Bible is filled with wisdom to help you overcome your RATS or Crazy-Maker syndrome. Everyone starts as a Crazy-Maker, and every STAR will sometimes make the mistake of slipping back into RATS or Crazy-Maker behaviour during a tribulation. Sometimes, STARs will devolve into RATS or Crazy-Maker due to some trauma in the natural world and loss of hope.

Matthew 16:24-26 (KJV) Then said Jesus unto his disciples, If any man will come after me, let him deny himself, and take up his cross, and follow me. For whosoever will save his life shall lose it: and whosoever will lose his life for my sake shall find it. For what is a man profited, if he shall gain the whole world, and lose his own soul? or what shall a man give in exchange for his soul?

2 Corinthians 3:5 & 12:9 (KJV) Not that we are sufficient of ourselves to think any thing as of ourselves; but our sufficiency is of God; And he said unto me, My grace is sufficient for thee: for my strength is made perfect in weakness. Most gladly therefore will I rather glory in my infirmities, that the power of Christ may rest upon me.

Loosely translated, the Holy Bible teaches that anyone who focuses on protecting their secrets will lose their spiritual freedom. Anyone who would let go of their secrets to follow Jesus will gain spiritual freedom.

The Holy Bible also teaches that much of the good stuff we would like to get out of life comes from God, so we need to release self-will and accept God's Will. It is not easy for an adult RATS or Crazy-Maker to grow up after they have come to depend on their coping strategies, but with God's Help, RATSs and Crazy-Makers can grow up to become STARs.

1 Samuel 16:7 (KJV) But the LORD said unto Samuel, Look not on his countenance, or on the height of his stature; because I have refused him: for the LORD seeth not as man seeth; for man looketh on the outward appearance, but the LORD looketh on the heart.

Psalm 34:18 (KJV) The LORD is nigh unto them that are of a broken heart; and saveth such as be of a contrite spirit.

Isaiah 66:2 (KJV) For all those things hath mine hand made, and all those things have been, saith the LORD: but to this man will I look, even to him that is poor and of a contrite spirit, and trembleth at my word.

1 Peter 5:5 (KJV) … be clothed with humility: for God resisteth the proud, and giveth grace to the humble.

The Holy Bible teaches that God knows our hearts and will help those who are humble (not proud) in spirit. If your boss, your company's Human Resources department, or your significant other has rightfully accused you of being a RATS or Crazy-Maker, this book can help you. If someone has told you that you are a RATS or Crazy-Maker, you first need to consider the possibility that they are correct. Then, you need to determine if you are a RATS or Crazy-Maker or the victim of gaslighting from a RATS or Crazy-Maker. To be certain of your determination, you need to compare your behaviour with the principles of the Holy Bible. Only God, a psychotherapist, or a counsellor can help you determine what is true.

Psalm 34:18 (KJV) The LORD is nigh unto them that are of a broken heart; and saveth such as be of a contrite spirit.

Psalm 147:3 (KJV) He healeth the broken in heart, and bindeth up their wounds.

Ezekiel 36:26 (KJV) A new heart also will I give you, and a new spirit will I put within you: and I will take away the stony heart out of your flesh, and I will give you an heart of flesh.

The Holy Bible teaches that God will save you, give you a new spirit, and help you grow into a STAR.

If you have determined that you are a RATS or Crazy-Maker, the first thing that you need to do is confess it to yourself and to God. *If* your RATS or Crazy-Maker behaviour has hurt someone, and *if* you would like to apologize to repair the relationship, *then* you need first to identify the sufferer's *primary personality style* and *then* tailor your apology to their primary personality style.

If you hurt someone with your RATS primary personality style, you cannot atone for your trespass using your RATS primary personality style. If you attempt to atone for your trespass with your RATS primary personality style, they might misinterpret your apology as another attack. This misinterpretation might transform the sufferer into a RATS or Crazy-Maker.

If you hurt someone with your RATS primary personality style, you must apologize in their primary personality style so that they can comprehend and appreciate the apology.

If you are a RATS or a Crazy-Maker, psychotherapy or counselling will be very helpful in overcoming your RATS Syndrome or Crazy-Maker Syndrome. However, nobody can help you overcome the syndrome better than our divine God-head.

1 John 4:18 (KJV) There is no fear in love; but perfect love casteth out fear: because fear hath torment. He that feareth is not made perfect in love.

The divine Godhead will fill you with so much divine love that it will eliminate anxiety, worries, and low self-esteem. Divine love will eliminate the RATS Syndrome or Crazy-Maker Syndrome from your character.

If a RATS or Crazy-Maker struggles with change, it is almost always true that Satan's pride is holding them back from admitting that they need help and holding them back from turning to God in their time of need.

Nothing within Man's World is strong enough to conquer the causes of anxiety and distress of things produced in Man's World. Only our divine Godhead can reach into Man's World from God's Kingdom of Heaven to give us the strength to stand strong.

It is important to remember that God is a Redeemer, not a Rescuer. God will help you through the tough times but will not remove the tough times from your path. God will help you prepare for your STAR growth but will not write your exams. God will guide you to know what is correct but will not make your decisions for you. No matter what happens to you in Man's World, God is there to help you through the storm if you accept God's Help.

Introduction to Biblical Duties

This section is for relationships that can confront and deal with the conflict *safely*. *If* there is any possibility or evidence of physical abuse or any form of danger, *then* you need to walk away from the conflict location and, if desired, attempt to resolve the conflict issue from a safe distance.

I will not claim that RATS are always evil, but they are always emotionally draining.

2 Timothy 3:12-17 (KJV) Yea, and all that will live godly in Christ Jesus shall suffer persecution. But evil men and seducers shall wax worse and worse, deceiving, and being deceived. But continue thou in the things which thou hast learned and hast been assured of, knowing of whom thou hast learned them; And that from a child thou hast known the holy scriptures, which are able to make thee wise unto salvation through faith which is in Christ Jesus. All scripture is given by inspiration of God, and is profitable for doctrine, for reproof, for correction, for instruction in righteousness: That the man of God may be perfect, throughly furnished unto all good works.

Revelation 13:11 (KJV) And I beheld another beast coming up out of the earth; and he had two horns like a lamb, and he spake as a dragon.

The Holy Bible cautions us to be careful who we pay attention to. All scripture is given by inspiration from God to help people who choose to follow God. There will always be evil men and seducers who will claim to be like Jesus but speak evil like Satan, the dragon.

Ephesians 4:29 (KJV) Let no corrupt communication proceed out of your mouth, but that which is good to the use of edifying, that it may minister grace unto the hearers.

Romans 8:28 (KJV) And we know that all things work together for good to them that love God, to them who are the called according to his purpose.

Philippians 3:12-14 (KJV) Not as though I had already attained, either were already perfect: but I follow after, if that I may apprehend that for which also I am apprehended of Christ Jesus. Brethren, I count not myself to have apprehended: but this one thing I do, forgetting those things which are behind, and reaching forth unto those things which are before, I press toward the mark for the prize of the high calling of God in Christ Jesus.

The Holy Bible gives explicit rules about how we are to speak to each other.

Excellent Communication is always simple, but it is never easy. Communication is actually quite simple. All you have to do is follow the recipes found throughout the Holy Bible. However, communication is never easy because we live in a fallen world; we are not Kingdom of Heaven STARs, and we will inevitably make mistakes, resulting in misunderstandings that result in disagreement and/or conflict. We need to forgive ourselves for our mistakes and refocus on the prize of the high calling of God in Jesus Christ.

James, the natural brother of Jesus, has much to say on this topic in the Book of James in the Holy Bible.

1 Corinthians 13:11 (KJV) When I was a child, I spake as a child, I understood as a child, I thought as a child: but when I became a man, I put away childish things.

Philippians 4:8 (KJV) Finally, brethren, whatsoever things are true, whatsoever things are honest, whatsoever things are just, whatsoever things are pure, whatsoever things are lovely, whatsoever things are of good report; if there be any virtue, and if there be any praise, think on these things.

These recipes for dealing with conflict are found throughout the Holy Bible. The teaching of 1 Corinthians 13:11 seems to hint that a person's growth is from Crazy-Maker to RATS to STAR. Rules are typically easy for Technical P-Style to follow after they decide which rules to follow.

More instructions and teachings will follow in a later chapter entitled Relationship Rules from the Holy Bible.

One Life and Then Judgment

Hebrews 9:27-28 (KJV) And as it is appointed unto men once to die, but after this the judgment: So Christ was once offered to bear the sins of many; and unto them that look for him shall he appear the second time without sin unto salvation.

Luke 16:19-31 (KJV) There was a certain rich man, which was clothed in purple and fine linen, and fared sumptuously every day: And there was a certain beggar named Lazarus, which was laid at his gate, full of sores, And desiring to be fed with the crumbs which fell from the rich man's table: moreover the dogs came and licked his sores. And it came to pass, that the beggar died, and was carried by the angels into Abraham's bosom: the rich man also died, and was buried; And in hell he lift up his eyes, being in torments, and seeth Abraham afar off, and Lazarus in his bosom. And he cried and said, Father Abraham, have mercy on me, and send Lazarus, that he may dip the tip of his finger in water, and cool my tongue; for I am tormented in this flame. But Abraham said, Son, remember that thou in thy lifetime receivedst thy good things, and likewise Lazarus evil things: but now he is comforted, and thou art tormented. And beside all this, between us and you there is a great gulf fixed: so that they which would pass from hence to you cannot; neither can they pass to us, that would come from thence. Then he said, I pray thee therefore, father, that thou wouldest send him to my father's house: For I have five brethren; that he may testify unto them, lest they also come into this place of torment. Abraham saith unto him, They have Moses and the prophets; let them hear them. And he said, Nay, father Abraham: but if one went unto them from the dead, they will repent. And he said unto him, If they hear not Moses and the prophets, neither will they be persuaded, though one rose from the dead.

2 Peter 1:2-11 (KJV) Grace and peace be multiplied unto you through the knowledge of God, and of Jesus our Lord, According as his divine power hath given unto us all things that pertain unto life and godliness, through the knowledge of him that hath called us to glory and virtue: Whereby are given unto us exceeding great and precious promises: that by these ye might be partakers of the divine nature, having escaped the corruption that is in the world through lust. And beside this, giving all diligence, add to your faith virtue; and to virtue knowledge; And to knowledge temperance; and to temperance patience; and to patience godliness; And to godliness brotherly kindness; and to brotherly kindness charity. For if these things be in you, and abound, they make you that ye shall neither be barren nor unfruitful in the knowledge of our Lord Jesus Christ. But he that lacketh these things is blind, and cannot see afar off, and hath forgotten that he was purged from his old sins. Wherefore the rather, brethren, give diligence to make your calling and election sure: for if ye do these things, ye shall never fall: For so an entrance shall be ministered unto you abundantly into the everlasting kingdom of our Lord and Saviour Jesus Christ.

Luke 16:19-31 teaches why we should do our best to become Kingdom of Heaven STARs. Since nobody can know the exact moment of their death, everyone should start as soon as possible to implement the wisdom of the Holy Bible. The benefit is that the sooner you implement the wisdom of the Holy Bible, the sooner you will reap the rewards and blessings promised in 2 Peter 1:2-11.

Section 5 – From the Bible